KING ASHOKA THE GREAT

KING ASHOKA THE GREAT

SUNDARAM DUBEY

INTRODUCTION OF THE LEGENG

Ashoka 304 – 232 BCE), popularly known as Ashoka the Great, was an Indian emperor of the Maurya Empire, son of Bindusara, who ruled almost the entire Indian subcontinent from c. 268 to 232 BCE. Ashoka promoted the spread of Buddhism across ancient Asia.

LIFE OF THE LEGEND

An Eventful Life Introduction Ashoka, one of the greatest rulers of India, stands out in ancient history as the only ruler who had a genuine respect for human life. He was a man of great wisdom and strength of character. He was a great man not only because of what he achieved, but also because of his personal qualities. Ashoka became an Emperor in 273 BC, about 2250 years ago. He ruled over a vast kingdom which stretched from the Hindu Kush mountains in the west, to the foothills of the Himalayas in the North and Madras in the South.

Pataliputra was the capital of Ashoka's Empire. In the first five years of his reign, Ashoka behaved like the other rulers of the day. He kept a splendid court and ruled like a despot, without bothering about the advice of others or thinking about the effect of his commands on the people. His favourite pastimes were hunting, feasting and war.

He killed thousands of beasts during royal hunts and he gave very little thought to the lives of his subjects. In the ninth year of his reign, Ashoka decided to conquer Kalinga, a kingdom in the region of present-day Orissa. A fierce battle took place and more than 1,00,000 people were killed and An Eventful Life 3 1,50,000 taken prisoners. Ashoka was horrified and shocked by the terrible destruction and death which took place during the battle.

Although he won the battle, Ashoka felt very unhappy. This may not seem surprising to you because many conquerors throughout history have felt unhappy over the deaths that have occurred during their conquests. But Ashoka was the only one who had the courage to publicly admit his mistake. Not only did he announce his feelings of grief and regret, he vowed that he would never go to war again. Soon after the Kalinga War, Ashoka became a Buddhist.

He obeyed the rules of conduct laid down in the Noble Eightfold Path, which were to use right vision, right thoughts, right speech, right action, right livelihood, right efforts, right mindfulness and right concentration to achieve true salvation and liberty. He also followed the rules of 'dharma' preached by Lord Buddha, such as obedience to one's father and mother, respect for life and avoidance of violence.

Ashoka's greatness lies in not only setting a personal example for everyone to follow but also in taking practical steps to ensure that the rules he had laid down would benefit the common man throughout his vast Empire. Ashoka stopped killing of certain animals for food such as parrots, porcupines and tortoises. Besides, he prohibited killing for sport, which was the favourite pastime of the nobility of that time. He stopped the killing of peacocks and deer for his own kitchen.

Ashoka took practical steps to see that the rules of 'dharma' were observed by all his people and that they understood its meaning. He appointed officers to discuss and explain the principles of 'dharma' to the people. Not only did he insist that his subjects follow these principles, he personally set an example for all to follow. One of the important steps Ashoka took to announce his new way of life was to send missionaries to preach Buddhism to far corners of his Empire.

They were sent to Kashmir, Ceylon, Nepal and even Egypt. He had many inscriptions carved on pillars and rocks across his kingdom to explain and lay down rules of behaviour. Ashoka's teachings inscribed on rocks and pillars can 4 Ashoka, the Great be seen even to this day. And India has adopted Ashoka's wheel as an emblem in our national flag. Where other great Kings sent generals to conquer men's bodies, Ashoka sent monks to conquer men's minds. Ashoka reigned for about forty years

. Apart from the Kalinga War, they were years of peace for India. Ashoka governed by kindness rather than by force. Throughout his immense kingdom there was prosperity, contentment and happiness.

Not even the Mughal Emperors like Akbar or Aurangzeb controlled such a large part of India, nor have conditions of life ever been as good as in Ashoka's day. Ashoka worked hard for the benefit of the people. He set up roads, planted shady banyan trees by the side of the roads, dug wells, constructed free rest-houses and hospitals in his vast Empire. Before Ashoka's reign Buddha's teachings had not spread beyond India. Ashoka was responsible for spreading Buddhism throughout the eastern world. He sent missionaries to other countries and he himself showed how Buddhism could be applied in everyday affairs and the affairs of a large Empire.

It is surprising that such a powerful King decided to give up wars of conquest. He devoted all his energy towards making his people happy. Herein lies the greatness of Ashoka. He was a man of character who lived by all he preached and did not expect others to do what he did not do himself. In the annals of kingship there is scarcely any record comparable to that of Ashoka, both as a man and as a ruler.

To bring out the chief features of his greatness, historians have instituted comparisons between him and other distinguished monarchs in history, eastern and western, ancient and modern, Pagan, Muslim, and Christian. In his efforts to establish a kingdom of righteousness after the highest ideals of a theocracy, he has been likened to David and Solomon of Israel in the days of its greatest glory; in his patronage of Buddhism, which helped to transform a local into a world religion, he has been compared to Constantine in relation to Christianity; in his philosophy and piety he recalls Marcus Aurelius; he was a Charlemagne in the extent of his Empire and, to some extent, in the methods of his administration, too, while his Edicts, "rugged, uncouth, involved, full of repetitions," read like the speeches of Oliver Cromwell in their mannerisms.

Lastly, he has been compared to Khalifa Omar and Emperor Akbar, whom also he resembles in certain respects. As in the case of great characters like King Arthur and his Knights of the Round Table, the good King Alfred, or King St. Louis of France, a mass of tradition has gathered round the name of Ashoka.

Myths and legends have freely and luxuriantly grown round it, especially in the tropical climate of Ceylon, and it would have been very difficult to recover his true history, were it not for the fact that he has himself left us a sort of autobiography in his messages to his people, written on rocky surfaces or exquisitely finished and polished pillars of stone.

In these sermons-on stone we find his true self revealed and expressed, his philosophy of life, his conception of an Emperor's duties and responsibilities, and the extent to which he lived to realise the high ideals and principles he professed and preached. This kind of evidence, which is not only a contemporary but a personal record, too, is unique in Indian history, and, whether suggested by indigenous or foreign precedents, it is fortunate we have it for one of our greatest men.

"O that my words were written! That they were graven with an iron pen and lead in the rock for ever!" This pious wish of Job was more than realised in the case of Ashoka in a series of thirty-five inscriptions published on rock or pillar, of which some are located at the extremities of his Empire. Family Background Of the two sources of his history, the legends (whether Ceylonese or Indian) rather hover over his early life and stand to retreat before the light of the edicts thrown upon his later life, his career as Emperor.

The two sources are, again, sometimes in agreement, but oftener in conflict, in which case the inscriptions, as personal and contemporary documents, will have to be preferred.

HISTORY OF THE LEGEND

Moreover, the legends are themselves at conflict with one another in many places, and thus betray themselves all the more. Ceylon tradition (as narrated in the Dipavamsa and the Mahavamsa) makes Bindusara the husband of sixteen wives and father of 101 sons, of whom only three are named, viz., Sumana 6 Ashoka, the Great (Susima according to the northern legends), the eldest, Ashoka, and Tisya (uterine brother of Ashoka), the youngest son.

The mother of Ashoka in the northern tradition is Subhadrangi, the beautiful daughter of a Brahmin of Champa, who bore Bindusara another son named Vigatashoka (Vitashoka), and not Tisya of the Ceylon books. In the southern tradition she is called Dharma, the principal Queen (aggamahesi), the preceptor of whose family was an Ajivika saint named Janasana—a fact which may explain Ashoka's patronage of the Ajivika Sect.

Dharma came of the Kshatriya clan of the Moriyas. According to established constitutional usage, Ashoka as Prince served as Viceroy in one of the remoter provinces of the Empire. This was the province of Western India called Avantirattham (Mahabodhivamsa) with headquarters

(Rajadhani) at Ujjain in the Ceylon tradition, but in the Indian legends it is the kingdom of the Svasas in Uttarapatha with headquarters at Taxila, where Ashoka was temporarily sent to supersede Prince Susima and quell the revolt against his maladministration.

There was a second rebellion at Taxila which Prince Susima failed to quell, when the throne at Pataliputra fell vacant and was promptly seized by Ashoka with the aid of the minister, Radhagupta, and subsequently held deliberately against the eldest brother who was killed in the attempt to dethrone the usurper (Divyavadana).

But the story of the accession is somewhat differently told in the Ceylonese legends, which make Ashoka seize the throne from Ujjain, where he had been throughout serving as viceroy, by making a short work of all his brothers except Tisya. The northern and southern legends, however, agree as regards the disputed succession, which may therefore be taken as a fact. The southern legends are far wide of the truth in making Ashoka a fratricide, the murderer of 99 brothers for the sake of the throne, for which he is dubbed Chandashoka. Senart has well shown how the legends themselves are not at one in their account of Ashoka's career of cruelty, Taranath makes Ashoka kill only six brothers.

Other authorities do not attribute to him any murder at all, but other forms of cruelty. The Ashoka-avadana represents him as killing his officers and wives, and setting up a hell where some innocent people are subjected to the most refined tortures. The Mahavamsa An Eventful Life 7 also relates how his minister under his instructions decapitates some false monks till he is stopped by his brother.

In the Ashokaavadana, he sets a price upon the heads of Brahmin ascetics who insulted the statue of the Buddha till he is checked by his brother, Vitashoka. Yuan Chwang records the tradition of "Ashoka and his Queen, in succession, making determined efforts to destroy the Bodhi Chinese traveller, I-tsing, according to which Ashoka's sovereignty was propnesied by the Buddha himself. The tradition relates that King Bimbisara once saw in a dream that a piece of cloth and a gold stick were both divided up into eighteen fragments which, as explained by the Buddha, symbolised the eighteen schools into which his teaching would be split "more than a hundred years after his nirvana, when there will arise a King named Ashoka, who will rule over the whole of Jambudvipa".

The Buddha's prophecy about Ashoka as a righteous King who will enshrine his bodily relics in 84,000 "dharmarajikas" occurs in the Divyavadana, tree," and when each attempt failed and the tree grew up each time, "Ashoka surrounded it with a stone wall". According to Fa-hien, the Queen tried to destroy the Bo-tree out of jealousy when Ashoka, already a zealous Buddhist, was always to be found under that tree for worship.

The fact is that these legends were out to emphasise the contrast between the criminal career of Ashoka prior to his conversion and his virtuous conduct that followed it. They were interested in blackening his character to glorify the religion which could transmute base metal into gold, convert Chandashoka into Dharmashoka, and make of a monster of cruelty the simplest of men! The epithet Chandashoka suggested by Ashoka's earlier cruelties does not, however, seem to be justified, if we limit his cruelties only to the murder of a single brother in the contest for the throne, while it may be that the brothers referred to as being alive well on in his reign might be only his uterine brothers, of whom the legends give the name of one, viz., Tisya.

The number of brothers slain according to the legends may be an exaggeration which marks legends, and even the edicts of Ashoka. It may be well assumed, too, that the brothers slain might have been his stepbrothers. According to the Mahabodhivamsa, as already stated, these 98 brothers with their leader, Yuvaraja Sumana, were slain in the course of the war of succession they had forced on Ashoka, 8 Ashoka, the Great whom they regarded as the usurper. Thus Ashoka could not be held responsible for their death under such circumstances.

"Sons and grandsons", who were all maintained at royal expense. Pillar Edict VII contains the expression: "In all my female establishments, both here (at the capital) and in the outlying towns". Besides the evidence showing the existence of the harems of his brothers at different provincial towns, we have also the evidence of such brothers (called kumaras and aryaputras) serving as his Viceroys at headquarters named, viz., Taxila, Tosali Ujjaini and Suvarnagiri. These Viceroys could not be his Sons. Lastly, his affection for his children, too, expresses itself in the Kalinga Edict I: "I desire for my children that they may enjoy every kind of prosperity and happiness both in this world and in the next" A man with such tender solicitude for the welfare of all his relations could not be a monster of cruelty, as the legends represent him to be. The relations between Ashoka and his younger brother appear to be quite friendly and natural in the legends, but they give different accounts of these relations.

Yuan Chwang, calling him Mahendra, relates that he used his high birth to violate the laws, lead a dissolute life, and oppress the people, till the matter was reported to Ashoka by his high ministers and old statesmen. Then Ashoka in tears explained to his brother how awkward was his position due to his conduct. Mahendra, confessing guilt, asked for a reprieve of seven days, during which, by the practice of contemplation in a dark chamber, he became an arhat and was granted cave-dwellings at Pataliputra for his residence. According to Fa-hien, Ashoka's brother, whose name he does not mention, had retired to the solitude on a hill which he was loath to leave, though "the King sincerely reverenced him and wished and begged him to come and live in his family where he could supply all his wants." In the end, the King constructed for him a hill inside the city of Pataliputra to live closer to him. A different story is, however, given in other works.

The Pali works call him Tisya, the Divyavadana Vitashoka, and some Chinese works Sudatta and Sugatra. These works also specify his offence to be that, as a Tirthika, he had slandered the professed Buddhists as living in luxury and subject to passions. To convince him of his error, Ashoka conspired with An Eventful Life 9 his chief minister to place him on the throne, and then appeared suddenly to accuse him as a usurper, whom he condemned to die after seven days. During this time he was treated to all pleasures and luxuries for which, however, he had no taste, with death facing him.

By this example, Ashoka wanted to show that no Buddhist with his dread of death and birth could ever give himself to pleasures. He then set free Vitashoka, who, however, went away to a frontier land, became an arhat, saw Ashoka at Pataliputra, but soon left for another district where he was beheaded, being taken for one of the Nirgranthas upon whose heads the local King set a price. In the Mahavamsa, Ashoka appoints his brother Tisya as uparaja, his Vice-regent, but he retired as a religious devotee under the influence of the Yonaka preacher, Mahadharmaraksita; and was known by the name of 'Ekaviharika, a vihara being excavated for him at enormous expense in the rock called Bhojakagiri by Ashoka according to the story given in Dhammapala's comment on the verses composed by Ekaviharika in the Theragatha Commentary. The same work refers to the youngest brother of Ashoka, called Vitashoka, whom it treats evidently as not the same brother as—Tissa Ekaviharika.

It relates how he grew up, mastering all the vidyas and silpas, arts and sciences, prescribed for the study of Kshatriyakumaras; then he became a householder, and, under his teacher, Giridatta Thera, mastered the Sutra Pitaka and Abhidhamma Pitaka, until one day, while at shaving (massu-kamma), he noticed in his mirror his grey hairs, which set him a-thinking of the decay of life, and he at once embraced monkhood under Giridatta and soon became an arhat. This particular text thus distinguishes between the two brothers of Ashoka by their different teachers, and attributes to them different gathas. Some of the Edicts mention the names of his closer relations. Thus the second Queen Karuvaki is mentioned, together with her son, Prince Tivara. A later inscription mentions Ashoka's grandson Dasharatha. Both legends and inscriptions are at one in making Ashoka a polygamist.

The chronicles make his first wife the daughter of a merchant of Vedisagiri, Devi by name, whom Ashoka had married when he was Viceroy at Ujjain. The Mahabodhivamsa calls her Vedisa-mahadevi and a Shakyani or a Shakya-kumari, 10 Ashoka, the Great as being the daughter of a clan of the Shakyas who had immigrated to "Vedisam nagaram" out of fear of Vidudabha menacing their mother-country (Vidudabhabh-ayagatanam Sakiyanam avasam Vedisam). Thus the first wife of Ashoka was related to the Buddha's family or clan. She is also described as having caused the construction of the Great Vihara of Vedisagiri, probably the first of the monuments of Sanchi and Bhilsa (taya karapitam Vedisagirimahaviharam).

This explains why Ashoka selected Sanchi and its beautiful neighbourhood for his architectural activities. Vedisa also figures as an important Buddhist place in earlier literature (Sutra Nipata). Of Devi were born the son, Mahendra, and the daughter, Sanghamitra, who was married to Ashoka's nephew, Agnibrahma, and gave birth to a son named Sumana, According to Mahavamsa, Devi did not follow Ashoka as sovereign to Pataliputra, for there his Chief Queen (agramahisi) then was Asandhimitra.

The Divyavadana knows of a third wife of Ashoka, Padmavati by name, them other of Dharmavivardhana, who was afterwards called Kunala. Both Mahavamsa and Divyavadana agree in mentioning Tissarakkha or Tisya-raksita as the last Chief Queen of Ashoka.

The Divyavadana mentions Samprati as Kunala's son. The Kashmir Chronicle mentions Jalauka as another son of Ashoka, Fa-hien mentions Dharmavivardhana as a son of Ashoka, whom he appointed as the Viceroy of Gandhara. Thus, taking the legends and Edicts together we find the following relations of Ashoka: Father: Bindusara, who had many wives. Mother: Subhadrangi, as named in the northern tradition; also called Dharma in the southern tradition.

Brothers: (1) Sumana or Susima, eldest, but stepbrother; (2) Tisya, uterine and youngest brother; also called Vitashoka or Vigatashoka in the northern legends, Mahendra by Yuan Chwang, and Sudatta and Sugatra in some Chinese works; (3) Vitashoka, according to Theragatha Commentary. Wives: (1) Devi, with her full name, "Vedisa-Mahadevi Shakyakumari"; (2) Karuvaki, called "Dvitiya devi Tivalamata," "second Queen, mother of Tivara" in the Edict; (3) Asandhimitra, designated as agramahisi, Chief Queen; (4) Padmavati; (5) Tisyaraksita. An Eventful Life 11 Sons—(1) Mahendra, son of Devi; (2) Tivara, son of Karuvaki; (3) Kunala, son of Padmavati, also known by the name of Dharmavivardhana, as mentioned in Divyavadana, and by Fahien; (4) Jalauka, mentioned in the Kashmir Chronicle.

The Edicts tell of four Princes serving as Viceroys in four different, and remote, provinces, and designated as Kumaras or Aryaputras, as distinguished from the sons of a lower status called dalakas from the status of their mothers. Daughters—(1) Sanghamitra, whose mother was Devi; (2) Charumati. Sons-in-law—(1) Agnibrahma, husband of Sanghamitra; (2) Devapala Ksatriya, married to Charumati Grandsons—(1) Dasharatha, who became King; (2) Samprati, son of Kunala; (3) Sumana, son of Sanghamitra. On the basis of the texts to which we owe most of these names, it is also possible to ascertain some dates in the domestic life of Ashoka. For instance, we are told in the Mahavamsa that Ashoka's eldest son and daughter, Mahendra and Sanghamitra, were both ordained in the sixth year of his coronation when they were respectively twenty and eighteen years old.

Taking the date of Ashoka's coronation to be 270 BC, we get 284 BC and 282 BC as the dates of the birth of Mahendra and his sister respectively. If we take the father's age at the birth of his eldest child as twenty years, then Ashoka must have been born in 304 BC and was thus seen by his august grandfather, Chandragupta Maurya, who died in 299 BC It is also stated that Ashoka's son-in-law, Agnibrahma, was ordained in the fourth year of his coronation, i.e., in 266 BC, before which a son was born to him. Thus Sanghamitra must have been married in 268 BC at the latest, i.e., at the age of fourteen.

Parentage, Brothers and Sisters The inscriptions of Ashoka throw no light on his early life and parentage. His brothers and sisters along with other kith and kin find mention in R. E. V in connection with the distribution of charities from their households by the Dharmamahamatras. Ashoka introduces them in such a manner as to suggest that they were persons who ranked with him in family relationship, and 12 Ashoka, the Great that they had their family establishments in Pataliputra and outlying towns.

The Pali tradition speaks of just one sister of Ashoka to whose son, Prince Agnibrahma, was married his daughter Sanghamitra and to whom she bore a son called Sumana. The Pali Chronicles expressly tell us that King Bindusara married sixteen wives by whom he had one hundred and one sons. Amongst them, Ashoka was second to none but Sumana, the eldest of all The Divyavadhana names the eldest son of Bindusara as Susima. Ashoka's only uterine brother was Tishya who is called Vigatashoka or Vitashoka in the Divyavadhana, and Sudatta or Sugatra in some Chinese works. The Theragatha contains two psalms, one attributed to the Thera Ekavihariya and the other to another Thera named Vitashoka.

The scholiast Dhammapala identifies Ekavihariya with Ashoka's brother Tishya and the second Thera with Ashoka's another brother Vitashoka, and represents them as two different individuals. This identification is not at all borne out by the earlier Canonical legends in the book of Apadana, and may therefore be dismissed as pure invention. According to the Pali narrative, when Ashoka seized the throne of Magadha, taking advantage of his father's old age and illness, his ninety-nine stepbrothers made a common cause with Sumana Susima who was the rightful heir to the throne and were all slain with him. The Tibetan historian Taranatha "makes Ashoka kill only six brothers" while in the Divyavadhana the fratricidal battle is described as one fought only between Susima-Sumana and Ashoka. Susima's defeat was mainly due to the lack of support from the ministers of his father who were all up against him.

The substance of truth in these legends seems to be that Ashoka's succession was a disputed one, which, however, has no corroboration from his records. The evidence of Ashoka's inscriptions may be construed in a sense to run counter to the trend of the Buddhist stories. In R. E. V, engraved not later than the 13th or 14th year of abhisheka, Ashoka mentions their brothers as having their family establishments in Pataliputra and outlying towns. On the other An Eventful Life 13 hand, in P. E. VII, engraved in the 27th year of abhisheka, he replaces his brothers by other Princes of the blood royal ranking with his sons in family relationship. The inference which may reasonably be drawn from this is that in the course of thirteen years his brothers either died or retired from the world.

According to Pali legends, Ashoka appointed his uterine brother Tishya-Vitashoka as uparaja or vice-regent. After Tishya had joined the Buddhist Order, the offer went to Ashoka's nephew and son-in-law Agnibrahma, and when he too joined forthwith the Buddhist Order in the fourth year of Ashoka's abhisheka, the office of the vice-regent went a begging. If reliance be placed upon the Pali account, there was no brother of Ashoka left after the 4th year of his abhisheka to function as his viceroy. But the preamble or forwarding note of the three Isila or Northern Mysore versions of M. R. E., probably engraved not earlier than the 26th year of abhisheka, seems to suggest that the fact was otherwise. The Isila copy of the edict in question was to be forwarded to the Mahamatras of the place under the authority of the Aryaputra and the Mahamatras stationed at Suvanjagiri, which was evidently the headquarters of the southern viceroy. If the forwarding note of the Isila versions were despatched by Ashoka, as seems more probable, by Aryaputra (Ayaputa) Ashoka could not but have meant a brother of his.

If locally drafted at Suvarnagiri, as would seem less likely, by Aryaputra one must understand just a son of Ashoka.

As for Ashoka's early life, the Buddhist story as narrated in the Dipavamsa has nothing to say beyond the fact that he was the second son of Bindusara and a grandson of Chandragupta of the Maurya family, or that his personal name was Priyadarshana, meaning "one of amiable mien", "one whose handsome appearance was comparable to that of the moon". According to the same authority, Ashoka and Priyadarshin were the names or titles assumed by Priyadarshana at the time of his two consecrations.

The Divyavadhana story, on the contrary, says that Ashoka was the name of the Prince given him by his father at the instance of his mother. Furthermore, the Sanskrit legend goes to represent him as a person of ugly appearance and fierce nature 14 Ashoka, the Great evidently to build thereupon the grotesque and repulsive story of how he came to pass as Ashoka the Wicked. The earlier Pali account, met with whether in the Dipavamsa or in the Samanta-pasadika and Mahavamsa, is silent on Ashoka's mother. The Mahavamsatika introduces us for the first time to his mother Dharma (Pali Dhamma) who was a princess from the Maurya clan of Kshatriyas (Moriyavavamsaji) and whose family preceptor was an Ajivika named Janasana, Jarasana or Jarasona. She is represented as the chief Queen of Bindusara.

She is called Subhadrangi in the Avadanamala. The Divyavadhana story does not name her but certainly represents her as "the beautiful daughter of a Brahman of Champa." Jealous of her excessive beauty, the Queens of Bindusara made her do the work of a female barber. Highly pleased with her work, the King granted her a boon, which she availed of by asking him to marry her. Satisfied with her social position which she disclosed, the King made her his chief Queen.

The Divyavadhana legend, too, associates an Ajivaka named Pingalavatsa with Ashoka's mother. Precisely as in the Pali story, Ashoka received him with due honour when his prediction about his succession came true. In the Mahavamsa-tika, Bindusara's mother is said to have been Chandragupta's eldest maternal uncle's daughter whom he married. The tradition is a late one and of a very doubtful character. It is very strange indeed that none of the Indian legends says anything of the daughter of Seleucus Nikator who gave her in marriage to Chandragupta to make a matrimonial alliance with him.

It would have been a more interesting fact, if Bindusara were represented as a son of Chandragupta by his Greek wife. Predecessors and Pedigree: Ashoka, in his P. E. VII, speaks of the former Kings who had reigned in the long past and during several centuries, who too were the sincere well-wishers of their subjects, and by whom too various public works of a philanthropic nature were done.

He introduces them, however, just to throw into bold relief the ineffectiveness of the means and methods adopted by them, the insufficiency of the results obtained, and the lesser value of the works done as compared and contrasted with those adopted, obtained and done by him. An Eventful Life 15 Whom did he mean by these predecessors? Such expressions of his as atikamtam (in the long past), bhutapuve (formerly) and bahuni vasa-satani (during many hundred years) correspond to such introductory Jataka phrases as atite (in the past) and bhutapubbam. (bhutapurvam, “formerly”).

Going by this correspondence, one cannot but take it that Ashoka had within his mental purview rather the legendary monarchs noted for their righteous rule and noble deeds, such as those extolled in the Brahmanas, Aranyakas and Upanishads, the Sanskrit Epics, and the Canonical texts of the Jainas and Buddhists. Ashoka’s predecessors in the Magadha line of Kings belonged to five royal dynasties, to wit, (1) the Barhadratha or Brihadratha, (2) the Haryanka, (3) the Saisunaga or Shishunaga, (4) the Nanda, and (5) the Maurya (Pali Moriya). The Barhadratha dynasty founded by Brihadratha, son of Vasu Uparichara of the Chedi race and father of Jarasandha of the Great Epic fame, came to an end in the 6th century B. C., prior to the rise of Buddhism. The founding of the hill-girt city of Girivraja or Rajagriha is the notable work of this dynasty. The Barhadratha dynasty was followed at about the rise of Buddhism by the Haryanka, which latter is said to have come to an end seventy two years after the Buddha’s demise. Bimbisara, Ajatashatru and Udaya are the three successive rulers of this dynasty who are noted in history.

Amongst them, Bimbisara deserves to be honoured not only as the real founder of the Haryanka dynasty but also as that of the imperial power of Magadha. The Pali Nikayas credit him with the creation of some permanent land-endowments and royal fiefs in favour of certain Vedic colleges in his dominions. He is also known as the builder and donor of the Venuvana monastery at Rajagriha dedicated to the Buddha and his followers which was the first Buddhist monastery in India. He lent the service of his court-physician, Jivaka, to the Sangha and befriended the Buddha and his followers in various ways. He allowed his talented Queen Kshema to become a bhikshuni. It was indeed during his reign and in his dominions that many new movements of religious thought were started and fostered. In these respects, the name of his great contemporary, Prasenajit of Kosala, is equally noteworthy. 16 Ashoka, the Great Ajatashatru paved really the way for a further extension of the supremacy of Magadha in Northern India. It is evident from the Samannaphala Sutra that he occasionally met the well-known religious teachers and leading thinkers of the time to discuss the problem of importance.

Later Buddhist traditions credit him with the extension of patronage to the Buddhist Theras when they met at Rajagriha to hold the First Buddhist Council, as well as with the erection of a memorable stupa at a suburb of Rajagriha for the preservation of the bodily remains of the Buddha collected from the stupas erected by others. The Jainas claim that he greatly honoured Mahavira and his doctrine. Ajatashatru's son and successor, Udayi, is said to have transferred his capital from Rajagriha to Pataliputra, definitely in the fourth year of his reign, according to the Puranas. The Manjusri-mulakalpa would in vain have us believe that he committed the Words of Buddha to writing, though it may be true, as suggested, that he was able to effect a further extension of the supremacy of Magadha. Even as regards Udayi's grandson, Munda, it is stated in the Anguttara Nikaya and its Commentary that deeply grieved at the death of his beloved Queen, Bhadra, he sought solace through instructions from the Buddhist Thera, Narada, a fact which goes to indicate that in the matter of meeting holy persons of wisdom he followed in the footsteps of his forefathers. Ajatashatru and his successors earned, according to the Pali Chronicles, the notoriety of being patricides, and sick of it, the citizens deposed the last King of their line and replaced him by his popular minister Shishunaga.

Thus the Haryanka dynasty was supplanted by the Shishunaga. The Shishunagas ceased to rule one hundred and forty years after the Buddha's demise (c. 348 or 347 BC). The only King of this family, worthy of mention, is Kalashoka (Ashoka the Blackie), apparently the same person as Bana's Kakavarna Shishunaga. The Pali Chronicles relate that during his reign, just a century after the Buddha's demise, and under his royal patronage was held the Second Buddhist Council at Vaishali, which is not improbable. It may be noted here that the confusion made between Dbarmashoka An Eventful Life 17 and the crow-black Kalashoka was accountable for the Divyavadhana description of the former as a man of ugly appearance.

Even the Mahabodhivamsa records nothing noteworthy of the reign of Kalashoka's ten sons and successors whom it names. According to this later Pali Chronicle, his eldest son and immediate successor was

Bhadrasena. His ninth son, Nandivardhana, may be identified with his namesake in the Puranas, in which case his tenth or last son, Panchamaka, will figure as the same person as Mahanandi, the last King of the Shishunaga dynasty, according to the Puranas.

The Mulakalpa praises Visoka as a good King who worshipped Buddha's relics for 76 years, and his successor, Shurasena, who reigned for 17 years as a monarch who "caused stupas to be put up to the confines of the sea," which is evidently a baseless exaggeration. The Shishunaga dynasty came to an end with the rise of the Nandas into power one hundred and forty years after the Buddha's demise (c. 348 or 347 BC). Both the Pali Chronicles and the Puranas speak of nine Nandas, but they differ when the former represent them as nine brothers with a short reign of 22 years and the latter represent them as father and eight sons with a much longer reign of 40 (28 + 12) or 100 (88 + 12) years. The first King of this dynasty is Ugrasenananda according to the Mahabodhivamsa, and the last King Dhanananda

The Puranas name the first King as Mahapadmananda but leave his sons unnamed. The Greek writer Curtius speaks only of two Nandas, namely, Agrammes who was a contemporary of Alexander the Great, and whose father was a usurper of the throne, while the Mulakalpa speaks only of one Nanda who is said to have died at the age of 66. The traditional accounts differ as to how the Nandas came to replace the Shishunagas. According to the Mahavamsa-tika, the founder King of this dynasty accidentally fell into the hands of a gang of thieves and freebooters (chora) who used Malaya as their hiding place. He was a warrior-like man (yodhasadiso puriso). After the death of their leader he managed to secure their leadership and went on as theretofore to plunder villages and kingdoms. Pricked by conscience that such a life as this did not behove a 18 Ashoka, the Great warrior like him, he made up his mind to take a kingdom. He declared himself under the name of Nanda, and getting his brothers and people to side with him, seized a frontier town, the citizens whereof made an alliance with him instead of accepting his ultimatum.

In this very manner he gained the support of a large number of the inhabitants of Jambudvipa, and ultimately marched into Pataliputra. Thus he seized the kingdom of Magadha. But he was destined to die shortly after that. According to the Mulakalpa story, on the other hand, Nanda rose into power and gained the throne from a position of the Prime Minister, as though by a magical process. He was surrounded in his capital by the Brahman controversialists with false pride and big claims. Though pious and a man of judgement, the King gave them riches and did not deny them his patronage. But he had a Buddhist saint for his good spiritual guide under whose influence he became a believer in Buddha, honoured his sacred relics, and built 24 viharas. Vararuchi is represented as his Prime Minister, and Panini as his friend, a tradition to which Jayaswal attaches undue importance. The Puranas extol Mahapadmananda as an "extirpator of all kshatriyas" and as a "sole monarch bringing all under his sway".

The historical justification of this praise has been fully discussed by Raychaudhary. It may suffice here to add that the epithet Mahapadma is a numerical term, which is expressive of the enormous wealth of the founder of the Nanda dynasty. The signification of the Pali name, Dhanananda, of the last King of the family is the same. Raychaudhary rightly observes indeed when he says, "'The first Nanda left to his sons not only a big Empire but a large army and a full exchequer as well." None need be surprised, therefore, that Indian literature preserves the tradition of fabulous riches of a Nanda King. As for the last King, we read in the Mahavamsa-tika, "The youngest brother was called Dhanananda for his passion for hoarding wealth. He collected riches to the amount of eighty crores... Levying taxes even on skins, gums, trees and stones, he amassed further treasures which he disposed of similarly." The same authority also relates that Dhanananda built a danasala at Pataliputra, from which he gave away abundant riches to the Brahmans according to their seniority and ranks, a fact which An Eventful Life 19 finds mention also in the Mulakalpa account of King Nanda. The Mulakalpa has evidently mixed up the two accounts, namely, that of the first Nanda and that of the last.

With regard to the fall of the last Nanda King 140 years after the Buddha's demise, c. 326 or 325 B. C., the Mahavamsa and its tika on the one hand,

and the Puranas on the other show a complete agreement in so far as they attribute it to the machination of the "Brahman named Kautilya-Chanakya. The Mulakalpa alone suggests that the fall of the Nanda King was due to the alienation of the feeling of the whole body of ministers inadvertently caused by him. The tradition of extermination of the Nanda dynasty by Vishnugupta-Kautilya, is met with in the concluding verse of the Kautilya Arthashastra, the opening verses of the Kamandakiya Nitisara, as well as Vishakhadatta's Mudrarakshasa and the Mulakalpa. In the Mahavamsa and the Mulakalpa, Chanakya, the Prime Minister of Chandragupta Maurya, is described as "full of fierce wrath" (chandakkodhava), "successful in wrath, who was Death (Yamantaka) when angry."

The Mahavamsa-tika and the Mudrarakshasa give us slightly different stories of how Chanakya avenged the humiliation suffered by him at the hands of the last Nanda by using Chandragupta as a tool and established the latter in the throne of Magadha in c. 326 or 325 BC. In the Mahavamsa-tika Chanakya is described as an erudite, resourceful and tricky Brahman of Takshashila who was well versed in the Vedic lore, and an expert in the principles of polity. But his teeth being all broken, his face became ugly to look at. As a controversialist he came to Pataliputra, and as a Brahman leader he took his seat when King Dhanananda was distributing large gifts among the Brahmans. Disgusted with his uncomely sight, the King ordered his men to turn him out. Enraged by this, Chanakya pronounced his curse, saying, "In this earth bounded by the four seas let there no longer be the prosperity of the Nandas." This being reported, the King became very angry and ordered his men to arrest him forthwith.

Whilst trying to escape in the disguise of an Ajivika, he cleverly managed to evade the detection, though still inside the inner court of the royal residence. In the meantime he got hold of Prince Parvata whom he tempted with sovereignty, made good his escape together with the Prince and went to the Vindhya mountain. On looking out for a person who was worthy of sovereignty he chanced to see Prince Chandragupta of the Maurya family who was then being brought up in the family of a cowherd unaware of his royal origin.

He took Chandragupta to his retreat in the Vindhya mountain and trained him up. First he employed him to behead Prince Parvata and subsequently to collect treasures by plundering villages and towns. When he was thus able to prove his ability and to raise an army Chanakya set him to march to Pataliputra and seize the throne by putting Dhanananda to death. The connection of Chanakya with Takshashila is interesting. The explanation for the introduction of Parvatakumara in the story lies really in the Mudrarakshasa in which the machinations of Chanakya against Nanda were directed to conciliating Rakshasa, a minister of Nanda, and getting Malayaketu of Parvata as an ally.

The early career of Chandragupta it is necessary to watch in the light of the available Greek accounts his activities and position in the Punjab and Northwestern Frontier Provinces at the time of and immediately after Alexander the Great's invasion. And for the same the reader may be referred for the present to Raychaudhary's critical summary. As for the most notable events of the life and career of Chandragupta mention may be made of the following six: • The unification of all the states and fighting forces of Northwestern India beyond the Middle Country under his leadership. • The liberation of India from foreign yoke. • The overthrow of the Nanda power. • The defeat of Seleucus Nikator ending in a treaty by which the Greek general and successor of Alexander the Great ceded certain territories to Chandragupta and which was consummated by a matrimonial alliance. • The foundation of a mighty Indian Empire. •

The coming of Megasthenes as an ambassador of Seleucus Nikator to Chandragupta's court and capital. The account of India left by Megasthenes in his Indika is invaluable as presenting An Eventful Life 21 to us a contemporary picture of Chandragupta's palace, capital, kingdom, country, administrative system, etc. Chandragupta who is otherwise praised in the Malakalpa as 'a very prosperous lord of the earth', 'true to his word', and 'a man of pious soul' (mahabhogi satyasandhas cha dbarmatma sa mahipatih), is said to have killed many living beings on the advice of a bad spiritual guide (akalyanamitra.) He died after a successful reign of 24 years and was succeeded by his son Bindusara. According to the Mulakalpa legend, Bindusara was a minor when he was placed on the throne by his father. It is said that 'while a minor he obtained great comfort; when of full manhood he turned out to be bold, eloquent and sweet-tongued. He reigned for 28 years,—25 years according to the Puranas, and 70 years according to the Mulakalpa, which is improbable. Strangely enough, the Mulakalpa represents the wicked Chanakya as his Prime Minister.

The royal family in which he was born is called Nandarajakula instead of Maurya. One may just be amused by the ingenuity of the Mahavamsatika in the invention of stories to account for the etymological significance of the names, Chandragupta ("one who was guarded by a bull called Chandra") and Bindusara (one on whose body flowed the blood of she-goats"), both of which are far-fetched. The son and successor of Sandrokottos (Chandragupta) is known to the Greek historian Strabo by the name of Amitrochades, Allitrochades, and to Athenaios by that of Amitrachates equated by Fleet, and subsequently also by Jarl Charpentier, with Amitrakhada (Devourer of enemies) which is traceable in literature as an epithet of Indra. Raychaudhary still sticks to his equation with Amitraghata, a term which is met with in Patanjali's Mahabhashya and corresponds to Amitranam hanta in the Aitareya Brahmana. The following two facts are really important to be noted: (i) That Ptolemy Philadelphos, King of Egypt, sent Deimachos as his ambassador to Bindusara; and (ii) That, according to the Dipavamsa and Samantapasadika, Bindusara was a votary of the Brahmans and a staunch supporter of the Brahminical sects.

Social Status: The barber story is almost proverbial in the ancient royal tradition of India. When a reigning monarch was found stingy in the payment of rewards or in making gifts, he was taken to be a barber's son. There must have been some such reason at the back of the Brahminical tradition regarding the Shudra origin of the Nandas and Mauryas. The Puranas predict, "As son of Mahanandin (the last Saisunaga) by a Shudra woman will be born a King, Mahapadma (Nanda) who will exterminate all kshatriyas. Thereafter Kings will be of Shudra origin." The founder of the Nanda family is called 'the leading vile man' (nichamukhyah) in the Mulakalpa (verse 424). In the Mahavamsa-tika the first Nanda, who was a warrior-like man, figures, as we saw, as the powerful leader of a gang of thieves and a band of freebooters. He is not, however, connected by the Pali tradition with the last Saisunaga through blood-relationship The Mulakalpa legend says that originally he was the Prime Minister of the last King of Visoka's family. Curtius narrates a story from an Indian source, which is devised to account for the Shudra origin of Agrammes (Augrasainya Nanda). According to this story, father of Agrammes was a wretched barber, who could be in love-intrigue with the Queen of the reigning King because of his prepossessing appearance.

By her influence he gained so much confidence of the King as to figure ultimately as a trusted adviser. Taking advantage of this privileged position, he treacherously murdered the King, and 'under the pretence of acting as guardian to the royal children, usurped the supreme authority, and having put the royal young Princes to death begot Agrammes. The suggestion is that the Nanda contemporary of Alexander was a barber's son by the Queen dowager of the last Saisunaga. Hemachandra in his Parisishtaparvan, however, represents the first Nanda 'as the son of a courtezan by a barber', while, according to the Puranas, he was 'a son of the last Saisunaga by a Shudra woman.

The process of myth-making did not stop short there; the Shudra or barber story continued. Despite the fact that neither the Pali Chronicles nor the Puranas suggest any blood-connection between the Nandas and the Mauryas, Vishakhadatta in his Mudrarakshasa, describes Chandragupta not only as Mauryasuta but also as Nandanvaya (one belonging to the Nanda dynasty). "Kshemendra and Somadeva refer to him as Purvananda-sutra. The commentator on An Eventful Life 23 the Vishnu Purana says that Chandragupta was the son of Nanda by a wife called Mura, whence he and his descendants were called Mauryas. Dhundiraja, the commentator on the Mudrarakshasa, informs us on the other hand that Chandragupta was the eldest son of Maurya who was the son of the Nanda King Sarvarthasiddha by Mura, daughter of a Vrishala Shudra. In the Mudrarakshasa itself Chanakya addresses Chandragupta as a Vrishala or Shudra.

Mr. C. D. Chatterjee rightly points out to me that the derivation of the dynastic name Maurya as a matronymic from Mura is grammatically incorrect; it may be treated as a patronymic from Mura. It is untenable also on the ground that according to the Vishnu Purana and the Arthashastra, the child takes the caste of its father, whether born of conjugal wedlock or not. The force of the story of the barber mother or grandmother of Chandragupta may be counteracted by the Divyavadhana story of the barber-mother of Ashoka himself. His mother was not a woman of the barber caste but a very handsome and accomplished Brahman girl from Champa whom other Queens of Bindusara, jealous of her, employed her in the palace to attend on the King as a female hairdresser. When she disclosed the real fact to the King, she said, "Lord, I am not a barber girl but a daughter of a Brahman by whom I am offered to be your wife.

Hemchandra in his Parisishtaparvan, derives the name Maurya from mayura (peacock) and suggests that Chandragupta came to be styled Maurya from the circumstance that he was "the son of a daughter of the chief of a village of peacock-tamers.If the Greek writer Justin describes Sandrocottus as a man "of mean origin", it does not mean much, since he must have based his account on an Indian tradition. The Pali Chronicles, on the other hand, and Buddhist legends generally represent Chandragupta as a scion of the Moriya clan of kshatriyas, the Moriyas of Pipphalivana. Led, however, by a Shakya-phobia, the Buddhist legends describe the Moriyas as descendants of the Shakyas who fled away from their own territory when it was overrun by the army of Vidudabha-Virudhaka, the usurper King of Kosala, and founded a new territory. The story is guilty of anachronism because, as borne out by the Mahaparinibbana Suttanta, the Moriyas of Pipphalivana were, precisely like the 24 Ashoka, the Great Shakyas of Kapilavastu, one of the eight rival claimants for the bodily remains of the Buddha. As for the connection of the Mauryas of Pataliputra with the Moriyas, the Mahavamsa-tika tells us that Chandragupta's mother who was the chief Queen of the then reigning Moriya King fled in disguise from the Moriya capital to Pushpapura (Pataliputra) during her advanced pregnancy, and gave birth to her son there when the Moriya territory was seized by a powerful neighbour (samantaranna).

CONECTIONS

The story built up in this connection reads somehow as a later replica of the earlier legend of the birth of Ashoka's elder stepbrother's son Nyagrodha, and at the root of the ingenuity of the one, precisely as at that of the other, is a fantastic philological justification of the personal name. Chandragupta does not appear to have been known to Megasthenes, and, for the matter of that, to most of the Greek writers, as a scion of the Maurya family. None need be surprised at all if the connection of the Mauryas with the Moriyas was due to an after-thought on the part of the Buddhists when they wanted to especially honour their Dharmashoka and claim him as their own man. The Buddhist legends concerning the Shakya lineage of the Moriyas or Mauryas would seem accountable also for the representation of the Mauryas in certain late medieval Mysore inscriptions as Kshatriyas who sprang from Mandhatri of the solar race. Hemchandra, as we noted, accounts for the dynastic name Maurya by the tradition that Chandragupta was a son of the daughter of the headman of a village of mayuraposhakas (peacock-tamers). The Mahavamsa-tika which connects Chandragupta with the Moriyas, accounts for their name also by a tradition averring that they built in their capital 'peacock palaces that were filled and resounded with cries of peacocks.

In support of the connection of the Mauryas with peacocks, Raychaudhary notices the following two facts which create but a presumptive evidence: • That Aelian speaks of tame peacocks that were kept in the parks attached to the Maurya palace at Pataliputra and • That figures of peacocks were employed to decorate some of the projecting ends of the architraves of the east gateway as Sanchi. An Eventful Life 25 If any light is thrown on this point by Ashoka's R. E. I, it is rather this, namely, that the Mauryas of Pataliputra were inordinately fond of peacock's flesh. All the animals could be dispensed with and exempted from daily slaughter in the royal kitchen for the purpose of curry but not two peafowls. In other words, the

Mauryas were rather mayarakhadakas than mayaraposhakas. The figure of a peacock carved on the lower part of Ashoka's pillar at Rampurva does not necessarily indicate that the peacock was the emblem of the Mauryas, It may at the most be interpreted as a cognizance of Pipphalivana, which was the fatherland of the Moriya race of kshatriyas. There is no conclusive evidence as yet to establish Chandragupta's lineal descent from the Shakya-Moriyas or Nandas.

Plutarch's remark that "Androkottus himself, who was then a lad, saw Alexander himself and afterwards used to declare that Alexander might easily have occupied the whole country, as the then King was hated by his subjects on account of his mean and wicked disposition" must be taken with a grain of salt. There was nothing in Chandragupta's conversation to enrage Alexander who, according to Justin, 'did not scruple to give orders to kill the intrepid Indian lad for his boldness of speech'. It was quite against the youthful spirit of Chandragupta who in Justin's opinion was the brave hero and military leader to make India free, shaking off 'from its neck the yoke of slavery' since Alexander's death. To me Chandragupta was a man of the Uttarapatha or Gandhara, if not exactly of Takshashila. His early education, military training, and alliances were all in that part of India.

He added the whole of the province of Gandhara and the surrounding tribal states (in the Punjab and N. W. Frontier Provinces) to the growing Magadha Empire together with the territories ceded to him by Seleucus Nikator. The love was never lost between this aparanta and the Mauryas. Some at least of Ashoka's scribes were all persons whose habitual script was Kharoshthi, and a few of his artists were those who were still carrying on the tradition of the architecture of Persepolis. Chandragupta and Ashoka of the Maurya dynasty who could create a glorious history for themselves and their country did not need credentials based upon royal lineage. The Greek writers speak only of one matrimonial alliance by which Seleucus ratified his treaty with Chandragupta. 26 Ashoka, the Great Early Life There is hardly any educated person in India who has not heard of Ashoka and his stone inscriptions. Ashoka, he knows, was a Prince of the Maurya dynasty and grandson of Chandragupta, the

Sandrakottos of the Greek writers and, for some time, a contemporary of Alexander the Great.

The inscriptions of this monarch, he again knows, have been found all over India. But he may not be aware of their contents and may not know what account they furnish of that Maurya King. There are, no doubt, some Buddhist works, which set forth his life and work, but their trustworthy character has been rightly called in question. They mention many stones, which represent him to have been Kalashoka or Black Ashoka before, and Dharmashoka or Pious Ashoka after, his conversion to Buddhism. As the one aim of these works is to eulogise Buddhism by showing how it transformed Ashoka the Ogre into Ashoka the Pious, a suspicion naturally crosses our mind in regard to the correctness of their account. Such is not, however, the case with his epigraphic monuments, which being contemporary records and engraved by his orders, are of undoubted veracity. Nay, as we go through them, we feel as if his voice is still speaking to us and confiding what is passing in the innermostnecesses of his mind. The story of Ashoka that is being narrated is based almost entirely on these monuments, and we can be pretty certain that our account is not fiction, but history. What kind of records has Ashoka left behind him? Are they sufficiently numerous and important in details? These records, as we know, are all engraved on stone. They have been inscribed either on rocks or pillars or in caves.

Ashoka's rock inscriptions, again, are of two kinds: namely, (i) the Fourteen Rock Edicts, and (ii) the Minor Rock Edicts. The former are called Fourteen Rock Edicts, because they together form a set of fourteen different inscriptions following a serial order, and have been found in seven different localities— all on the confines of India, at any rate, of his Empire. The Minor Rock Edicts consist of two different records. They are inscribed together only in the three copies found in Mysore; in all other places, which are no less than four, Edict I only has been engraved. Ashoka's Pillar Inscriptions also may be distinguished into two An Eventful Life 27 classes: (i) Seven Pillar Edicts, and (ii) the Minor Pillar Inscriptions. The former of these constitute a group, but the latter are four different epigraphs. The Cave Inscriptions of Ashoka are, of course, those engraved in caves in the

Barabar Hills of Bihar. These are altogether no less than thirty-three different inscriptions throw light on a number of points connected with Ashoka, his administration, his religious faith, his missionary operations, and so on.

A careful comparison of these records is just what is needed in order to obtain the maximum that is knowable and historically acceptable about Ashoka. Those who have studied these epigraphs know full well that they profess to have emanated from a King who calls himself Piyadarshi, that is, Priyadarshin. When they were first being deciphered, now about three-quarters of a century ago, by James Prinsep to whom must go the credit of having unravelled the mystery of the Brahmi lipi, he was very much puzzled by the name Priyadarshin. He did not know who this Priyadarshin was, to what dynasty he belonged, and in what age he flourished. Soon thereafter, however, Tumour, who belonged to the Ceylon Civil Service, and was himself a great Pali scholar, identified Priyadarshin with Ashoka. He pointed out that the Sinhalese chronicle, the Dipavamsa, gave Piyadarshi or Piyadarshana as but another name of Ashoka, grandson of Chandragupta, the founder of the Maurya dynasty.

This identification, it is true, has not since then been called in question, but it was definitively demonstrated only nine years ago when the sixth copy of Minor Bock Edict I was discovered at Maski in the Raichur District, Nizam's Dominions. For this inscription mentions the name of Ashoka clearly and in the very first line. It is not therefore possible now to doubt that Priyadarshin and Ashoka are one and the same person, and that the author of these inscriptions is really the grandson of Chandragupta, who founded the Maurya Empire. We thus see that the author of our epigraphic records was known both as Ashoka and Priyadarshin. It was customary for the Kings of ancient India to have more than one name, of which one was their proper individual name and the others epithets or birudas as they are called. One of these two appellations must have been the personal name of the King, and the other his epithet.

And 28 Ashoka, the Great it appears that Priyadarshin was his epithet, for we know that Ashoka's grandfather, Chandragupta, has also been styled

Priyadarshana like him in one of the Ceylonese chronicles. Nobody can doubt that Chandragupta was his individual name. Priyadarshana or Priyadarshin must, therefore, be taken to be the biruda or secondary name. We know that this epithet in the case of Ashoka was Priyadarshin, and it is quite possible that Priyadarshin and not Priyadarshana was the biruda of his grandfather also. For in later times we find grandfather and grandson belonging to the same dynasty adopting the same biruda. The Ceylonese chronicles style Ashoka not only Priyadarshin but also Priyadarshana, taking the two words apparently in one and the same sense. And as from Ashoka's inscriptions we find that he was known really as Priyadarshin and not Priyadarshana, it is natural to presume that his grandfather also was Priyadarshin, not Priyadarshana. It is curious that this records call him Ashoka, only once, and Priyadarshin, in all other places

But instances are not wanting of Kings being known almost invariably by their epithets. Thus the son of Govinda III of the Rashtrakuta family of Manyakheta is known to us from all the documents so far only by his epithet, Amoghavarsha. We are somewhat better in regard to the author of our inscriptions. For one record at least gives his personal name, Ashoka. In most of his inscriptions Ashoka styles himself Devanampriya Priyadarshi Raja. This is the fullest appellation of the King. But sometimes the formula is abbreviated by the omission of one or two of these components. Thus we find Ashoka designated also Devanampriya Priyadarshi, Priyadarshi Raja, Devanampriya Raja, or even Devanampriya merely. The second component of Ashoka's full name is Priyadarshin, which we have just considered. Literally it means ' one of amiable look,' and may be freely rendered by one who is of gracious mien.' When and why he adopted this epithet we do not know, but certain it is that he used it almost as his personal name. We had better not, therefore, translate it, but leave it as it is. It is worthy of note that although Ashoka was a supreme ruler, he designates himself simply Raja. The grandiloquent titles, Maharaja and Rajadhiraja, employed singly or conjointly, had not come into use in Ashoka's time. What is more worthy of note is that he calls himself Devanampriya, and An Eventful Life 29 one can well understand how the modern students of Grammar (vyakarana) may feel inclined to laugh at it.

For do not Bhattoji Dikshita, author of the Siddhantakaumudi, and Hemachandra, author of the Abhidhanachintamani, tell us that Devanampriya means 'a fool' or 'dunce'? They are, therefore, apt to wonder what Ashoka means by calling himself Devanampriya. But it is to be noted that though this word has now a derogatory sense, it was not so originally, and especially in the time of Ashoka. Patanjali, we know, associates this word with bhavat, dirghayus, and ayushmat. This shows that like these honorific terms Devanampriya was employed as an auspicious mode of address or characterisation. Now, if we turn to Rock Edict VIII of Ashoka, we shall find that for Devanampriya of some versions we have rajano of others. This means that Devanampriya was an auspicious mode of address used with reference to Kings. And, as a matter of fact, the Dipavamsa applies the appellation Devanampriya to Tissa, the ruler of Ceylon and contemporary of Ashoka, and often employs it alone to denote that King. Epigraphic records also point to the same conclusion.

Thus in the Nagarjuni Hill Cave inscriptions, the term Devanampriya is used to designate a King called Dasharatha, who has been taken to be the grandson of Ashoka. Similarly, an epigraph from Ceylon gives this epithet among other Kings to Vankanasika-Tissa, Gajabahuka-gamini, and Mahallaka-Naga. Devanampriya was thus an auspicious mode of address or honorific characterisation, before the Christian era, confined to the Kings only, and was so used probably to indicate the belief that the rulers were under the protection of the gods (devas). The term had therefore be better translated by " dear unto the gods," or " beloved of the gods." Ashoka's full royal style was thus " King Priyadarshin, beloved of the gods." Many of Ashoka's inscriptions commence with the formula: Devanampriya Piyadarshi Raja evam aha, " thus saith King Priyadarshin, beloved of the gods." This has been rightly compared by Senart with the phrase with which the proclamations of the Achaemenides, from Darius to Artaxerxes Ochus, begin. One such instance is that Darayavaush kshayathiya, "thus saith the King Darius."

In both cases the form of address commences with a phrase in the third person, and what is further worth noticing is that this phrase is immediately followed by the use of the first 30 Ashoka, the Great person. Of course, nobody can now maintain that this formula was imitated by Ashoka directly from Persia, for, as a matter of fact, we know that this was one of the protocols of the royal chancery noticed by Kautilya in his Arthashastra and consequently prevalent before the time of Ashoka. But nothing precludes us from holding with the French savant that the Indians adopted the Persian protocol and that this adoption was due to the Achaemenian conquest and administration of northwest India. Wherever in his records Ashoka gives any dates, he counts the years from the time of his coronation.

This has led scholars to believe the Sinhalese tradition that Ashoka was crowned four years after his accession to the throne. But this tradition also tells us that after the death of his father, Ashoka seized the throne by massacring ninety-nine of his brothers, and spared only one, the youngest, namely Tishya. This story is, however, refuted by his inscriptions which speak, not of one brother, but of several, living and staying again not only in Pataliputra, his capital, but also in various towns of his Empire. And if this is found to be a fiction, it is not intelligible why we should hold fast to that part of the tradition which places his coronation four years after his seizing the throne. In fact, it is not at all clear how his dating certain events of his reign from his coronation is evidence of there having been an interval between his coronation and accession to the throne.

Again, in the Nagarjuni Hill caves there are at least three inscriptions which are dated immediately after the coronation of Dasharatha, grandson of Ashoka. Are we to suppose here also that because these records, in their dating, refer to Dasharatha's coronation, this event did not coincide with his coming to the throne and that some period must have elapsed between them? There is therefore no good reason to think that any long interval such as that of four years elapsed between Ashoka's coronation and his assumption of the reins of government.

It appears that Ashoka was in the habit of celebrating the anniversary of his coronation by the release of prisoners. This is inferrible from what he says at the end of Pillar Edict V. "By me, who am consecrated twenty-six years up till now," says he there, " twenty-five jail deliveries have been effected just in that period." As prisoners were released twenty-five times in the space of An Eventful Life 31 twenty-six years, it means that the twenty-sixth year of his reign had not elapsed but was running on when the Pillar Edict was promulgated. It thus seems that the dates which he specifies for the incidents of his life are current regnal years, and not expired, as has been taken by scholars. Kautilya in his Arthashastra lays down that the King shall prohibit castration and destruction of animal fetus on certain days. Among these he includes the days of the nakshatra of the King and the country. In Pillar Edict V, Ashoka speaks of castration and branding of animals, and specifies on what days he has prohibited them. Curiously enough, most of these days agree with those mentioned by Kautilya. And what is noteworthy is that here he specifies only two nakshatra days, namely, Tishya and Punarvasu

. One of these is most probably the nakshatra of the King and the other of the country. And the question must arise: which nakshatra is of the King and which of the country? It is worthy of note that the Tishya nakshatra has been mentioned also in the two separate Edicts of Dhauli and Jaugada. These edicts, we know, were intended by Ashoka solely for the exhortation and guidance of the officials of the newly conquered province of Kalinga, and he issues the order that they shall be recited every Tishya day for their benefit. Evidently, of the two nakshatras greater importance has thus been assigned to Tishya than to Punarvasu. This may be seen also from the fact that although in the usual list of the nakshatras Tishya comes after Punarvasu, it is placed prior to the latter, not once but twice, in Pillar Edict V. It is difficult to avoid the conclusion that as so much importance has been given to Tishya, that must be the nakshatra of the King. If this inference is correct, Punarvasu becomes the nakshatra of the country, by which, we suppose, we have to understand the country of Magadha.

The edicts of Ashoka are concerned with his Dhamma and the means he adopted to disseminate it. They naturally, therefore, throw a flood of light on his life and career after he became a Buddhist. But let us here try and see what little these records tell us about his earlier life, both in his private and public capacity. We have already seen that he had several brothers and sisters living till the thirteenth year of his reign, and that they were 32 Ashoka, the Great residing not only in Pataliputra but also in the mofussil towns. Of course, Ashoka had his avarodhana or closed female apartments. How many Queens he actually had we do not know. But he had at least two, for there is reference to his second Queen in one of his inscriptions. And the very fact that she had been designated Second Queen shows that the relative rank of the Queens had in his day been fixed. The name of this Second Queen was Karuvaki, and his son from her was Tivara. The object of the inscription is to ensure for this Queen the merit of any donation she might be pleased to make. In Pillar Edict VII Ashoka speaks of his having commissioned some of his officers to induce the members of his royal household to make gifts and to see to their proper organisation.

It is interesting to note what members of his family he mentions in this connection. Of course, he first speaks of himself and his Queens. But immediately after his Queens he makes reference to his avarodhana and tells us that its inmates were living not only at his capital but also in the provinces. Anybody who reads the passage carefully cannot but think that his Queens were not the only members of his avarodhana. Who could then be the other members? They cannot be the wives of his male relatives, for they cannot with propriety be called his avarodhana. Were they his left-handed wives? His avarodhana would thus comprise not only the Queens but also other Purdah ladies of lower status. This no doubt reminds us of the Sinhalese tradition that when Ashoka during his father's lifetime was viceroy at Ujjain, he formed connection with a lady of the Setthi caste, who resided at Vedisagiri, modern Besnagar near Bhilsa, and continued to reside there even when Ashoka seized the throne and his children by her accompanied him to his capital. This legend clearly confirms the inference deducible from the Pillar Edict that Ashoka had women other than Queens and that his avarodhana was not all in Pataliputra, but that some of its members stayed in the mofussil. In the same Pillar Edict and in continuation of the same subject, namely, the distribution of the charities of the Royal Household, Ashoka speaks of his own sons and other devikumaras.

The sons of Ashoka are thus distinguished from the latter. Who could the ' other devikumaras be? Most probably, Ashoka is here referring to the sons not of his An Eventful Life 33 own Devis or Queens but the Queens of his father and consequently to his non-couterine brothers. Again, how many sons Ashoka had we do not know. But he must have had at least four sons. In ancient times it was customary for a King to appoint his sons, as far as possible, as viceroys of the outlying provinces. And four such Princes we find mentioned in his epigraphic records, as being in charge of the four viceroyalties of Takshashila, Ujjaini, Suvarnagiri, and Tosali. Ashoka had at least four sons. To sum up, Ashoka had a very large family. He had several brothers and sisters staying not only at Pataliputra but also outside in the Empire. Some of them were certainly his couterine brothers, but there were also some, sprung, no doubt, from his father, but by different mothers. Ashoka had also his avarodhana or closed female apartments, not only in his capital but also in the provinces.

They were occupied not only by his Queens but also other women with whom he had connection. He had at least two Queens, one of whom was named Karuvaki, and at least four sons. But whether Tivara, son of Karuvaki, was one of them it is not possible to determine. We know very little of Ashoka's private life. His records shed very little light upon it. There is, however, one passage in Rock Edict VI which is interesting. This edict describes how often and at what different places be dispatched the business of his people. Here he tells us that he has arranged to dispose of it at all places and at all times so that no King prior to him ever did it. Naturally, therefore, he specifies the places where he formerly whiled away his time but where now he attends to their affairs. " This therefore, I have done," says he, "namely that at all hours and in all places— whether I am eating or I am in the closed female apartments, in the inner chamber (garbhagriha), with the stud (vraja), on horseback (vinita) or in pleasure orchards, the Reporters may report people's business to me." Evidently, therefore, when Ashoka had no business to dispose of and, of course, was not asleep, he was to be found at his capital either regaling in the dining hall, engaged with the inmates of his harem, chatting in his retiring cabin, or inspecting the royal stud, enjoying a horse ride, or beguiling his time in the orchards. What special tastes and fascinations he had developed or evinced in these matters we do not know, but we do know what articles of food gratified his palate.

Even when he was rigorously carrying out his programme of stopping the slaughter and injury to living beings, he made certain reservations in regard to his royal table. But even now when this document of Dhamma was written," says he in Rock Edict I, "only three animals were killed for curry, namely, two peacocks and only one deer, but even that deer not regularly. Even these three animals will not afterwards be killed." Ashoka here admits that although he has stopped the butchering of all other animals, he has allowed the killing of peacocks and deer to serve him with meat. Evidently, he was fond of the flesh of these animals. And as he says that the animal that was regularly butchered for his table was not the deer, but the peacock, it appears that he was inordinately fond of the peafowl. In this connection what Buddhaghosha says in his commentary on the Samyuttanikaya is worth noting. "To the people of the frontier provinces, ganduppadas are delicious, but they are abominable to those of the Middle Country. To the latter the flesh of a peafowl is delicious. It is, however, abominable to others." It is, therefore, no wonder if Ashoka, who was a native of the Middle Country, could not for a long time give up the eating of the peafowl flesh. We need not, however, harbour any doubt as to his having ultimately eschewed it, as promised in his edict, and thus turned a staunch vegetarian. In another inscription Ashoka gives us another glimpse into his private life.

Rock Edict VIII informs us that for a long time past Kings were in the habit of going out on vihara-yatras or pleasure tours, where they enjoyed chase and other similar diversions but that he has replaced these by Dhammayatras or tours for Dhamma since the tenth year of his reign when he visited Sambodhi, that is, the place where Buddha obtained enlightenment. What Ashoka gives us here to understand is that until the tenth year he, like all other Kings, used to go out on pleasure excursions, where he indulged in manifold diversions, the most pre-eminent of which, however, was hunting. We cannot have any clear idea of this vihara-yatra, as Ashoka gives us no details and as no account of it is also forthcoming from any work of literature. The Ashramavasika Parvan of the Mahabharata, no doubt, contains a reference to the vihara-yatras which Yudhishthira organised for enabling Dhritarashtra to forget the grief caused by the death of An Eventful Life 35 his hundred sons. But only one verse it gives to show what items constituted these vihara-yatras. " There," we are told, " the aralikas (jugglers), chefs, and singers of ragas and shadavas waited on King Dhritarashtra as in town." The programme of Dhritarashtra's pleasure trip thus consisted of music, dainties, and conjurer's tricks.

There is no mention of chase here, because an old and blind man like Dhritarashtra cannot be expected to take delight in chase. But as Ashoka speaks of chase only and tells us nothing of the other diversions when he adverts to vihara-yatras, it appears that hunting formed the most important feature of a pleasure excursion in his time. In fact, hunting was so much indulged in by the Kings that it was considered by some ancient writers on Hindu polity to be a vice which they were exhorted to avoid. Pisuna, for instance, condemns chase, because danger from robbers, enemies, wild animals, forest conflagration, fear of stumbling, inability to distinguish the cardinal points, and so on, are the evils associated with it. Kautilya, on the other hand, strongly recommends it, because according to him exercise, reduction of fat and bile, skill in aiming at stationary and moving bodies, knowledge of the minds of animals and of their ever-changing movements when they are enraged are the good points of chase. Some of these good points, we involved any kind of brutality or butchery to life. We shall now try to see what Ashoka was like in his capacity as King before he became a staunch missionary of Buddhism. Very little about him even in this capacity is known, and what little we know is from Rock Edict I. From it, it appears that like all other Kings Ashoka was in the habit of feasting and amusing his subjects, —probably a diplomatic move to keep his people pleased and satisfied. One mode of public entertainment that he practised was the celebration of the samaja. The samaja was of two kinds. In one the people were treated to dainty dishes in which meat played the most important part. In the other they were treated to dancing, music, wrestling, and other performances. The former was obviously a convivial melee. The latter was intended for the amusement of the people, and in this sense the samaja was synonymous with ranga or prekshagara, that is, the amphitheatre, and sometimes denoted ' the concourse of the people,' assembled there. All the instances of the samaja described in the Brahminical and the Buddhist literature show that they were intended to feast the palate or the eye and the ear of the people. There can be no doubt that the ancient Kings of India were in the habit of holding samajas.

Thus in the celebrated Hathigumpha inscription we are told that Kharavela, King of Kalinga, amused his capital-town by celebrating utsavas and samajas. Precisely the same thing is reported in a Nasik cave inscription to have been done by Gautamiputra Satakarni, a King of the Dekkan. And, in fact, Kautilya himself lays down that a King " shall imitate (the people's) attachment to the samaja, utsava, and vihara of their country or divinity." Both the kinds of the samajas seem to have been celebrated by Ashoka. But when he began to preach Dhamma, he naturally tabooed those where animals were slain to serve meat, as we may infer from Rock Edict I. As there was nothing in the other samajas for him to object to, he retained them, but slightly changed the character of the exhibition of the public spectacles. He no doubt must have provided such spectacles as would not only cause amusement to his subjects but also generate, develop and disseminate Dhamma amongst them. Reasons of state may also have dictated his taking another step in the same direction. In the same record Ashoka tells us that the slaughter of hundreds of thousands of animals was daily going on in the royal kitchen before the edict was promulgated. The case is precisely like that narrated in the Vanaparvan of the Mahabharata where we are informed that two thousand cattle and two thousand kine were slain every day in the kitchen of a King called Rantideva and that by doling out meat to his people he attained to incomparable fame.

And, in fact, the practice of daily doling out food to hundreds of people is still found in the Native States of India. Like Rantideva, Ashoka must have been in the habit of distributing meat among his subjects, and that his object in doing so must have been precisely the same, namely, that of making himself popular. But he put a stop to this terrible animal carnage, the moment his conscience was aroused and he commenced teaching Dhamma. We thus see what Ashoka was as a private individual and also as a King till he embraced Buddhism. The picture we have here is certainly not as lucid and full as we may desire, but we do An Eventful Life 37 obtain something which is reliable and not based on mere legend. We see what sort of family he had, what individual tastes and likings he possessed, and in what pursuits he engaged himself when he was free from his routine work as a ruler.

We also know what titles he assumed as King, how he began his royal career, and what measures he adopted to entertain his people and enlist their attachment. He also regularly celebrated the anniversary of his coronation by releasing prisoners from jails. This is all we know of him as ruler before he became a Buddhist, that is, till after the eighth year of his reign when he subjugated Kalinga. Whether the earlier part of his reign was uneventful or whether he had made similar conquests or not we do not know. The earliest event of his reign that we find referred to in inscriptions is his conquest of Kalinga, which roughly corresponds to the tract of land on the coast of the Bay of Bengal between the Vaitarani and Languliya rivers. He vividly describes the horrors and miseries of this war. " 1,50,000," says he, "were carried away (as captives); 1,00,000 were slain, and many times as many died."

These are the figures for Kalinga only, and do not include the casualties in the King's army. We thus have to note that even in such a small province as Kalinga, as many as 1,00,000 were killed on the battlefield, many times as many died as the result of burning and sacking, and, what is more, no less than 1,50,000 were seized as slaves. Surely, these are appalling figures for a tiny district like Kalinga, and indicate the extreme horrors of a war even in that ancient period when the weapons of destruction were not so diabolical and deadly as now. Soon after this war Ashoka was converted to Buddhism and began to preach Dhamma. And the remembrance of this war struck him with extreme and genuine remorse. When an unconquered province, says he, is being conquered slaughter, death and captivity must occur. This is regrettable enough. But what is still more regrettable is that among those who die, are slaughtered or are taken captive, there must be many who are devoted to Dhamma and that such contingencies to these men, again, must spell disaster and affliction to their friends, acquaintances, and relatives, who, though they themselves are safe, yet feel undiminished affection for them. "

This is the lot of 38 Ashoka, the Great all men and is considered regrettable by the Beloved of the gods." The language is instinct with personal feeling, and the rocks still echo across the ages the wail of a penitent soul. There can be no doubt that this was genuine remorse. For, when the edict was proclaimed, he had already commenced in that country a zealous protection, longing and teaching of Dhamma. When a territory is newly subjugated and is in an unsettled condition, the officers who are charged with proper administration and maintenance of peace there are apt to transgress the bounds of justice and mercy. Such transgressions did actually occur on the part of his officers, and we know from one of his inscriptions how severely he chastised them and what steps he took to prevent such excesses in the future. Nay, the inhuman and iniquitous nature of the war so much haunted his mind that he was even ashamed of engraving this edict in the Kalinga country.

There are two places in Kalinga where his Rock Edicts have been inscribed. But while the edict which describes his conquest of this province has been incised along with other Rock Edicts at all other places this alone has been omitted from the copies coming from Kalinga. Surely, remorse and sense of shame cannot further go. We may be pretty certain that Ashoka made no further conquests. But why he conquered and annexed Kalinga to his Empire, which was already very extensive, is not quite clear. It seems, however, that Kalinga was a thorn in the body politic of his dominions. From Rock Edict XIII we know that the provinces of Andhra and Parimda were included in his kingdom. Of these Andhra denoted roughly the country comprising the Kistna and Godavari Districts. As the capital of his Empire was Pataliputra, it is not unreasonable to suppose that it included the greater portion of modern Bengal. And this receives confirmation if my suggestion is true that Parimda was somewhere on the eastern outskirts of the Mauryan Empire, possibly in Bengal.

Kalinga was thus a sort of wedge driven into the body politic and might at any time conspire with the foreign Choda kingdoms which were to the south. For the safety and consolidation of his state it was thus absolutely necessary to conquer Kalinga and make his Empire one compact mass; and this he did. An Eventful Life 39 A year after his conquest of Kalinga he became a Buddhist. For one year he was lukewarm, but thereafter he became very strenuous in his exertions for the Dhamma, and the idea of becoming a Chakravarti Dharmika Dharmaraja haunted his mind. Supreme ruler of the earth ideal stimulated him to promote the temporal and spiritual good not only of his people but of the subjects of his independent neighbours, and not only of the human race, but of the whole animate world. We will take note of all his manifold activities, but shall first see what he did for his people as a ruler. For this, however, it is necessary to find out what the extent of his Empire was.

Physical Form and Personality The perfection of bodily form which goes into the make-up of kingly personality is regarded as another contributory factor. The ugly face with grim looks such as that of an owl is held as a positive disqualification. The Brahmans of India developed a popular science by the name of Mahapurusha-lakshanam or 'Characteristic bodily marks of a great man', and the Jainas-and Buddhists availed themselves of it in establishing the personal greatness of Mahavira and Buddha respectively. The Buddhist came to speak of the thirty-two major bodily marks and eighty minor characteristics. They were persuaded to believe along with the Brahman interpreters of the signs that a person endowed with these marks and characteristics is destined to become a righteous King overlord, if he remains in the world, or in the alternative, a perfect type of Buddha, if he renounces the world. The inscriptions of Ashoka have, however, nothing to say about his complexion and other details of his bodily form. In the Divyavadhana and other Sanskrit legends he is described as an ugly person with a repulsive appearance.

This delineation was due, as I sought to show, to confusion made between Ashoka the Pious and Ashoka the Blackie. The brightness and majesty of bodily form may shed lustre on man's personality but is not to be wholly identified with it. Buddha truly said to his disciple Vakkali, "What's the use looking at this rotten body! He who sees the doctrine, sees me, and he who sees me, sees the doctrine." A great man is indeed a great mind, which conceives and cherishes 40 Ashoka, the Great a grand ideal. It is precisely in this light that one should evaluate the greatness of Ashoka the man as well as of Ashoka the King. Education and Association: The Arthasastra expects the aspirant for kingship to be 'endowed with intelligence (buddhisampannah), possessed of intellect, talent, strong memory and keen mind (prajna-pragalbha-smriti-mati), trained in all sciences and arts (kritasilpah), and waiting upon the wise men of great experience (vriddhadarsi).

In the vriddha-samyoga, the same text enjoins that a Prince shall study the sciences and arts and strictly obey the discipline and rules imposed by them under the authority of his teacher. Having undergone the ceremony of tonsure, he shall learn the alphabet (lipi) and arithmetic (samkhyana), and after investiture with sacred thread, he shall study Vedic system (Trayi), and speculative philosophies (Anvikshaki) under the teachers of acknowledged authority (sishtebhyah), the science of wealth (Varta) under the government superintendents (adhyakshebhyah), and the science of government (Dandaniti) under the theoretical as well as practical politicians (vaktriprayoktyibhyah). To increase his efficiency in learning he shall ever keep up his contact with the experienced professors of sciences (vidyavriddha-samyogah). In the Lakkhana Suttanta, a righteous King overlord is expected to be a man of great wisdom, unsurpassed by others in the matter of knowledge, which is the ripe result of his waiting upon the eminent religious teachers with eagerness to learn from them the things that are conducive to human good.

In the Singalovada Suttanta, every man as a learner is required to serve well his teachers (acharya) by properly receiving the knowledge of the sciences and arts from them. In the case of King Kharavela, it is claimed in the Hathigumpha inscription that while a Prince, he had learnt the rules of writing, currency, accountancy, and law and become a master of sciences and arts (savavijavadata). We need not dwell here at length on the education of Indian Princes, sufficient information about which may be gathered from the later prasastis and literary works of all schools of thought. It may suffice for our immediate purpose to observe that the inscriptions of Ashoka indirectly throw some lights on his An Eventful Life 41 education and association. That he was familiar with the two main alphabets then prevalent in India, namely, Brahmi and Kharoshthi, is evident not only from the instructions issued as to the places where and the materials on which his inscriptions were to be incised, but also from the fact that he was aware of the errors committed by his scribes. His acquaintance with different local dialects and command over language is borne out by the inscriptions written obviously to his dictation.

His long stay in Western India and occasional mission to North Western India must have enabled him to be acquainted with the dialects of those places. From the forms of his inscriptions, it may be easily inferred that he was an adept also in the rules of royal writs. The inscriptions bear ample evidence to his sound knowledge of the principles of government. These bear a clear testimony also to his first-hand knowledge of the sacred texts and religious views of different sects. E.E. XII goes to prove that he personally met from time to time the exponents of different faiths and discussed various problems with them. In P.E. VI, he has laid due stress on the importance of going personally to wait upon the representatives of all sects. Waiting upon men of experience and wisdom for instructions and discussions looms large in E.E. VIII. In E.E. XII, he figures as a great lover of learning, healthy discussions and helpful debates. Wives and Children The Pali Chronicles and Samanta-pasadika tell us that while a Prince Ashoka married Devi, daughter of a banker, at Vidisha on his way to Ujjaini to join the office of the Viceroy (Uparaja) of Avanti.

The Mahavamsa-tika describes her as a very handsome and accomplished lady and names her father Deva. It is quite possible that, like Pushyagupta of the Junagarh rock inscription, Deva was a Rashtriya or Rashtrapala. In the Mahabodhivamsa, she is honoured as Vedisa-mahadevi, and represented as a Shakya Princess. It is said that after her marriage, she was taken to Ujjaini, where she bore him immediately a son called Mahendra, and two years later a daughter named Sanghamitra. She is said to have built a vihara at Vidisha for her son when he came to see her back en route to the island of Tamraparni. Devi stayed back at Vidisha but her children accompanied their father when he came back to 42 Ashoka, the Great Pataliputra and seized the throne. Sanghamitra was given in marriage to Prince Agnibrahma, a nephew of Ashoka, to whom she bore a son named Sumana. Agnibrahma, Sumana, Mahendra and Sanghamitra joined all the Buddhist Order. The above authorities offer us a systematic chronology of certain important events of Ashoka's reign in terms of the age of Mahendra. The Buddhist mission to Ceylon was led by Mahendra, and his sister, too, went over to the island when her services were needed for the "founding of an order of nuns there. The story of Devi and her children is conspicuous by its absence from the Sanskrit legends, The inscriptions of Ashoka are lacking in confirmation of its truth. In the edicts promulgated up till the 14th year of Ashoka's abhisheka we have no mention of his sons, his daughters being altogether out of the question. In his R. E. V, promulgated not earlier than the 13th year of abhisheka, he speaks of charities from the households of his brothers, sisters and others ranking with him in family relationship. He speaks indeed also of his different family establishments at Pataliputra and outlying towns. On the other hand, in his P. E. VII, engraved in the 27th year of abhisheka, his brothers, sisters and other kinsmen ranking with him go out of the picture, and his own sons (dalaka) and other Princes of the blood ranking with them are expressly introduced instead. The way in which they are mentioned leave no room for doubt that his sons were then grown up enough to make charities out of their own funds, though not exactly from their own family establishments (orodhas). His statement in P. E. VII is sufficiently explicit so as to make the meaning of that in E. E. V clear as to his own households. It goes to show that by his households or family establishments (to avoid the word harems) he chiefly meant his Queens (devis). The Queen's Edict contains his direction to the Mahamatras concerned as to how the donations and benefactions of his second Queen (dutiyaye deviye) Kaluvaki (Charuvaki or Kalavinka), mother of Tivala (Tivara), should be recorded or labelled with inscriptions, Thus the Queen's Edict clearly proves that Ashoka had at least two Queens at the time of its promulgation. Although the King's orders were issued to the Mahamatras everywhere (savata mahamata), it was engraved only on the pillar at

Kaushambi, a An Eventful Life 43 fact which may lead us to think that her residence was at Kaushambi, an outlying town. But Ashoka speaks of outlying towns, and not of one town only. Are we to understand from this that his Queens were not kept in one place, say, in his palace at Pataliputra, but at different towns, each having her separate establishment? The Pali tradition about the Vidisha residence of Devi favours the idea of there being separate family establishments for individual wives at different towns. But from Ashoka's statement, it does not necessarily follow that each establishment was allotted to one Queen. If Kaluvaki was his second Queen, who was his first or chief Queen? According to the Pali tradition, his beloved first Queen consort (piya aggamahisi) was Asandhimitta, a name, better title, which I am inclined to equate with Sk. Asandimitra (consort at the time of ascending the throne).

She died in the 26th year of Ashoka's abhisheka, and four years later Tishyaraksha was made his Queen consort. The Mahavamsa and Divyavadhana legends make her jealous of the Bo-tree on account of the King's fond attachment to it. The Divyavadhana legend which is unaware of her predecessor Asandimitra goes further to build up a most scandalous story of Tishyarakshita and her wrathful vengeance on Ashoka's favourite son, Kunala, when he was deputed to Takshashila to quell a revolt. The story of Tishyaraksha has no place in the Dipavamsa, nor even in the writings of Buddhaghosa. It must have grown up at a later period. Ashoka, as he appears in his inscriptions, could not have lost his sanity so much as to behave as a religious maniac with regard to the worship of the Bo tree as he has been represented to be. It is more reasonable to think and say that his wife by his side at the time of his coronation was the wife who accompanied him from Ujjaini, and she may be no other than the Vedisa-mahadevi. The Divyavadhana legend represents Ashoka's Queen Padmavati as mother of Kunala who was also known by the name of Dharmavardhana or Dharmavivardhana (the promoter of the cause of piety). The identity of Padmavati and Kaluvaki rests on the identity of their sons, Kunala and Tivala. Both Kunala and Tivala (Tivara) 44 Ashoka, the Great were nicknames.

As for the first, Mukherji rightly remarks that Ashoka first gave to Padmavati's newborn babe the name of Dharmavivardhana but on seeing the beauty of his eyes, as his amatyas, or ministers in attendance, pointed out were like those ' of the Himalayan bird Kunala, Ashoka nicknamed him as Kunala. He was called Dharmavivardhana because he was born when Ashoka had been reigning prosperously with righteousness. According to the Divyavadhana legend, he was born as soon as the 84,000 dharmarajikas were built, the 7th year of Ashoka's abhisheka being mentioned in the Pali Chronicles as the date of completion of the construction of the 84,000 viharas with chaityas. The name Tivala or Tivara, which is met with in a much later Indian inscription as the name of a King of Kosala, signifies a 'keen-eyed' hunter. Prince Tivala, too, was born when Ashoka had been prosperously reigning with righteousness. Successors: The Pali Chronicles and Samanta-pasadika do not carry the Maurya history beyond Ashoka. They create rather the impression that the whole glory of the dynasty vanished with him. His uterine brother Tishya-Vitashoka, son and daughter Mahendra and Sanghamitra, son-in-law Agnibrahma, and daughter's son Sumana joined the Buddhist Order. Nothing but the Buddhist religious edifices which he had built and the memory of other pious deeds performed by him remained to keep his name alive to posterity.

According to the Divyavadhana legend, Ashoka was succeeded by his grandson Sampadi, son of Kunala who was found unfit for the throne. Sampadi's lineal successors were Brihaspati, Vrishasena, Pushya-dharma and Pushyamitra. The last King of the family who began his career as a reactionary in favour of Brahmanism brought an end to himself and the Maurya dynasty by his ruthless act of vandalism directed to the destruction of the Buddhist viharas and stupas built and the killing of the Buddhist monks and nuns entertained by Ashoka. Jayaswal suggests that the Buddhist tradition of Pushyamitra is preserved also in the Mulakalpa account of the hostile action of Gomin who is said to have destroyed "monasteries with relics" and killed "monks of good conduct." An Eventful Life 45 The Buddhist tradition is misleading and inconclusive. Pushyamitra who, according to the Puranas, was the founder of the next dynasty, is represented as the last Maurya King and the lengths of the reign of Ashoka's successors are not given. Raychaudhary's critical summary of the history of Ashoka's Maurya successors seeks to build up a cosmos out of a chaos.

The Matsya Purana speaks of ten Mauryas whom it enumerates so clumsily as to make it uncertain whether by the" number ten it meant ten or seven successors of Ashoka. Some versions of the Vayu Purana definitely stand for nine successors, and try to reduce ten to the traditional number of nine Mauryas (nava Mauryah) by combining Bandhupalita and his son Indrapalita into one reign. The Vayu and Brahmanda Puranas speak of six successors who, together with the three first Mauryas, make up the traditional total of nine. In the circumstances one may reasonably question the accuracy of Raychaudhary's statement when he says, "The Matsya Purana gives the following list of Ashoka's successors: Dasharatha, Samprati, Satadhanvan and Brihadratha", inasmuch as their number, even together with that of the first three Mauryas, does not come up to the given total of ten (dasa Mauryah). The lengths of reigns suggested in the Matsya Purana as well as in some versions of the Vayu do not, when joined together, fit in with the traditional total length of 137 years.

Better in this respect is the position of the Brahmanda Purana as also of the Vayu, both of which give only 48 years as the total length of the reign of Ashoka's six successors. The Vishnu Purana list of six successors, viz., Suyasas, Dasharatha, Sangata, Shalisuka, Somasarman Shatadhanvan and Brihadratha may be reconciled to a great extent, as suggested by Raychaudhary, with that in the Matsya, if Suyasas and Sangata of the one be identified with Kunala and Samprati respectively of the other. Other names do not call for comment as these are mere passing shadows without any historical importance so far. The immediate successors of Ashoka was, according to the Divyavadhana legend, his grandson Sampadi (Samprati), and not his son Kunala, Kunala-Tivala or Kunala-Dharmavardhana whom Fa-hien distinctly mentions as the Viceroy of Gandhara. According 46 Ashoka, the Great to the Divyavadhana narrative, too, Kunala was deputed as his father's Vice-regent to Takshashila, the headquarters of the province of Gandhara. The Jaina author, Jinaprabhasuri claims Samprati, son of Kunala, as a great King who reigned in Pataliputra as an Emperor of India and founded viharas for the Jaina Shramanas ‘even in non-Aryan countries. Regarding Kunala and his immediate successor or successors, Raychaudhary observes: “Tradition is not unanimous regarding the accession of Kunala to the imperial throne. He is reputed to have been blind. His position was, therefore, probably like that of Dhritarashtra of the Great Epic and, though nominally regarded as the sovereign, he was physically unfit to carry on the work of government which was presumably entrusted to his favourite son Samprati, who is described by Jaina and Buddhist writers as the immediate successor of Ashoka.

Kunala’s son was Bandhupalita according to the Vayu Purana, Sampadi (Samprati) according to the Divyavadhana and the Pataliputra-kalpa of Jinaprabhasuri, and Vigatashoka according to Taranatha. Either these Princes were identical or they were brothers.” In the Gargi Samhita Salisuka is represented as a wicked King who had to abdicate the throne in favour of his virtuous elder brother, Vijaya. In deciding on the question of Ashoka’s successors, the ‘flashes of light that may be obtained from the ancient Indian inscriptions are as follows: • The Queen’s Edict which was probably engraved during the second period of Ashoka’s vigorous activity, 19th-21st year of abhisheka, mentions Tivala as his young son by his second Queen Kaluvaki. • In P. E. VII engraved in the 27th year of abhisheka, Ashoka speaks of the charities of his sons. • M. R. E. (Mysore copies), engraved probably in the 26th year of abhisheka, speaks of the Aryaputra Viceroy of Suvanagiri. • S. R. E. I, engraved probably in the 32nd year of abhisheka, speaks of three Kumara Viceroys stationed at Tosali, Ujjain and Takasila respectively.

An Eventful Life 47 • The Nagarjuni Hill-cave inscriptions record the three cavededications made by Dasharatha to the Ajivikas immediately after his consecration (anamtaliyam abhishitena). • The form of Brahmi letters employed in Dasharatha’s inscriptions indicates certain changes to account for which one must allow an interval of time, however short, between Ashoka and Dasharatha. The question arises—what was the course of action followed by the four Viceroys immediately after Ashoka’s death, if they had survived him as would seem most likely? The conflicting traditions, Buddhist, Jaina and Brahminical, serve to make confusion worse confounded instead of returning a satisfactory answer to this question. According to the Nagarjuni Hill-cave inscriptions, Dasharatha was a duly anointed King. From the situation of the caves dedicated by him, it is easy to infer that he was the sovereign of Magadha, better of Anga-Magadha. Vincent Smith had strong reasons to believe that Samprati's dominions 'included Avanti and Western India. But, as Raychaudhary points out, the Jaina writers represent him 'as ruling over Pataliputra as well as Ujjaini'. The tradition recorded by Jinaprabhasuri, however, describes Samprati as an Emperor of India whose capital, like that of Ashoka, was Pataliputra.

The hypothesis that Ashoka was succeeded by his two grandsons, Dasharatha and Samprati, by the first in respect of his eastern and by the second in that of his western dominions is 'little more than a guess' even on Vincent Smith's frank admission. If at a future date the veil be properly lifted from the history of Ashoka's successors, it will most probably be seen that no sooner had Ashoka passed away, no sooner had his strong hand been withdrawn than his four Viceroys asserted their independence, parcelling out his Empire into as many as four, if not more, separate principalities. Length of Reign and Last Days The length of Ashoka's reign since his abhisheka, which is evident from his dated inscriptions, consists of 27 years, while the 48 Ashoka, the Great same consists of 37 years according to the Pali Chronicles, and of 36 years according to the Puranas. Adding to the later 37 the earlier four years during which he reigned as an unanointed King since his accession according to the Pali tradition, we get the total length of his reign as comprising 41 years. It may be noted here that the Pali Chronicles and the Puranas give the same length of reign, namely, 24 years, to Chandragupta but slightly differ as regards the length of reign of Bindusara which, according to the former, is 28, and, according to the latter, 25 years. Correcting the Purana figure 25 to 28 and adding up the lengths of the three first reigns we get the total of 89. This total being added to the total length of 48 years of the reign of Ashoka's six successors, yields the traditional Purana figure of 137 years representing the duration of the Maurya dynasty of Magadha. If so, one has to discard the tradition of Ashoka's reign of four years as an unanointed King since his accession.

This tradition may be maintained if the duration of Bindusara's reign be accepted as 25 years and that of Ashoka's reign since coronation as 36 years, as suggested in the Puranas, in which case the required figure of 89 years may be obtained by adding up 24, 25, 4 and 36 years. The S.R.E. I and S.R.E. II represent the set of Ashoka's edicts which may be supposed to have been promulgated and engraved in the closing period of his reign. If he had followed the quinquennial system, the date of their promulgation cannot be earlier than the 32nd year of his abhisheka. S.R.E. I is addressed to the City-judiciaries of Tosali and Samapa. In it, they are taken to task for their failure in fully grasping the meaning and spirit of his instructions to them. They are urged not to cause oppression to his subjects by sudden arrest and coercion as well as summary trial. In it, he proposes to send forth every five years the Mahamatras under him on tours of inspection so as to check the miscarriage of justice. Here he modifies his quinquennial system and insists that the Kumara Viceroys at Tosali, Ujjain and Takasila should send forth on tours within every three years similar officials under them for the very same purpose. Thus this edict goes to suggest that highhandedness and arbitrary action of the City-judiciaries, particularly in the outlying provinces, served to cause annoyance to the people. An Eventful Life 49 Similarly S.R.E. II, which is addressed to the Viceroy-in-Council at Tosali and the Mahamatras who were Royal Commissioners at Samapa, presupposes hostile attitude and action of some of the 'frontagers' in violation of the terms of treaty or alliance. Whilst he wanted to assure them of his best intentions and friendliness, he did not omit to mention that he would tolerate them as long as their hostilities had not exceeded the limit of his patience.

The state of things as portrayed in these two edicts is faithfully represented in the Divyavadhana legend which, while giving an account of the last days of Ashoka, relates that the highhandedness and arbitrary action on the part of the officers in charge caused the citizens of the Uttarapatha to revolt (viruddha). On the arrival of the Kumara Viceroy, Kunala, at Takshashila, the citizens said, "We have revolted neither against the Kumara nor against King Ashoka, but the wicked ministers indeed come (here) and humiliate us." The Mahavamsa describes the last days of Ashoka as unhappy, and the Divyavadhana as both unhappy and tragic.

The causes of his unhappiness were, according to the Pali Chronicle, the death of his beloved Queen consort Asandimitra in the 26th year and the destruction of the Bo-tree out of jealousy by Tishyaraksha (rakshita) whom he appointed as Queen consort four years later. Over and above her attempt at the destruction of the Bo-tree, Tishyarakshita caused, according to the Divyavadhana legend, deep remorse to the King by her machination in getting the eyes of his beloved son Kunala plucked out after he had been deputed to Takshashila to quell a revolt in Uttarapatha. She is painted in the exaggerated Sanskrit story in the blackest of colours as a wily, passionate and revengeful woman of vilest character. Her story, which has happily no place in the earlier Pali Chronicle, Dipavamsa, was evidently developed, to heighten the glory of the Bo-tree as the living symbol of Buddha's enlightenment and Buddhism and the importance of its worship, as also to throw into bold relief the purity and magnanimity of the character of Kunala by a contrast with the vileness of the character of his stepmother. The Sanskrit legend on the strength of which Jayaswal placed much reliance goes a step further and introduces a pathetic episode of the virtual abdication of the throne by Ashoka.

 It is said that when Ashoka was about to exhaust the royal treasury by his over-extravagant subsidies to the Aryasangha or Sthavira Church, his Amatyas determined to put a stop- to it approached Sampadi, the heir apparent, and said, "King Ashoka, O Prince! who will live for a very short time is sending on this wealth to the Kurkutarama, but the treasury is the real strength to the Kings, so this (wreckless ruinous action of the King) must be stopped." Thereupon the Crown-Prince prevented the Steward (Bhandagarikah) from letting out any money from the treasury on the King's demand and instructed him to exercise a gradually restraining authority on all goods of value, even including metal plates, that might be given away as gifts to the Sangha. Thus the King was reduced to the position of a nominal ruler, although the administration was being carried on in his name until his death. Neither the amatyas nor the citizens, when asked by him, denied that he was all the time the supreme lord of the earth (prithivyam isvarah). Obviously this episode, too, was added to stress the significance of giving away everything, treasures, worldwide kingdom, wives and households, officers of the State, self and beloved son, by a powerful and benevolent monarch like Ashoka to the Buddhist Church for the sake of religion (kosham sthapayitva mahaprithivim antahpuramatya-ganam atmanam Kunalam charyasamghe niryatayitva).

But Ashoka was not so foolishly extravagant in his charities as to behave like that. Ashoka, however, speaks of his sons who were sufficiently grown up in the 27th year of his abhisheka to be able to distribute charities on their own account. From all the traditional sources, namely, the Pali Chronicles, the Divyavadhana, Kalhana's Rajatarangini and Taranatha's Tibetan history, one can collect names of just four sons of Ashoka, to wit, Mahendra who became a Buddhist monk, Kunala-Tivala who was deputed as a Viceroy to Takshashila, Jalauka who, as suggested in the Rajatarangini, was appointed the Viceroy or Governor of Kasmira, and Virasena who, according to Taranatha, "apparently wrested Gandhara from the hands of the feeble successor of the great Maurya at Pataliputra." The inscriptions of Ashoka themselves corroborate none of the three traditions regarding Mahendra, Jalauka, and Virasena. The truth of the tradition about Kunala being his father's Viceroy

An Eventful Life 51 at Takshashila is borne out by the evidence of S. R. E. I, which expressly refers to three Kumaras functioning then as Viceroys at Tosali, Ujjain, and Takasila, As long as any strong evidence is not forthcoming to prove the contrary, these Kumaras must be taken to represent Ashoka's three sons. Probably Tivala-Kunala was one of them. The problem of identification of the Kumara Viceroy of Gandhara may thus be solved by the legend of Kunala-Dharmavardhana. As regards the remaining two, we have still to grope in the dark, no light coming from traditions. And to add to the difficulty, the forwarding note of the Mysore copies of M. R. E. introduces us to an Aryaputra who was obviously functioning at the time as Viceroy at Suvarnagiri. He was certainly a brother or son of Ashoka. This is also a problem on which no further light can be thrown from any source. The giving away of the whole of the vast earth (kingdom, Empire) extending as far as to the seas and oceans with all its treasures by Ashoka in the name of religion and culture and their propounders and promulgators was but a formal affair with several ancient Kings of India who aspired to gain renown and popularity in this world. All that is possible to believe is that Ashoka virtually retired from active work of administration at his ripe old age, handing over its charge to the heir-apparent and ministers who might in the meantime have formed a conspiracy to upset the methods and policies initiated and followed by him. Proper Reign: The most vigorous period of Ashoka's reign commenced with the conquest of Kalinga in the 8th year of his abhisheka and ended with the promulgation of the two Separate Rock - Edicts probably in the 32nd year. The notable incidents of his reign, as far as these may be gathered from the inscriptions and legends, have been separately tabulated. They give rise to several problems which have been dealt with by previous scholars

WHAT THE WORLD KNOWS ANOUT THE INDIAN LEGEND IN DEEP

Sources of information Information about Ashoka comes from his inscriptions; other inscriptions that mention him or are possibly from his reign; and ancient literature, especially Buddhist texts.[15] These sources often contradict each other, although various historians have attempted to correlate their testimony. Plenty is known or not known. So, for example, while Ashoka is often attributed with building many hospitals during his time, there is no clear evidence that any hospitals existed in ancient India during the 3rd century BC or that Ashoka was responsible for commissioning the construction of any. Inscriptions Ashoka's inscriptions are the earliest self-representations of imperial power in the Indian subcontinent.However, these inscriptions are focused mainly on the topic of dhamma,

provide little information regarding other aspects of the Maurya state and society. Even on the topic of dhamma, the content of these inscriptions cannot be taken at face value. In the words of American academic John S. Strong, it is sometimes helpful to think of Ashoka's messages as propaganda by a politician whose aim is to present a favourable image of himself and his administration, rather than record historical facts. A small number of other inscriptions also provide some information about Ashoka.[16] For example, he finds a mention in the 2nd century Junagadh rock inscription of Rudradaman. An inscription discovered at Sirkap mentions a lost word beginning with "Priy", which is theorised to be Ashoka's title "Priyadarshi", although this is not certain.Some other inscriptions, such as the Sohgaura copper plate inscription, have been tentatively dated to Ashoka's period by a section of scholars, although others contest this. Buddhist legends Much of the information about Ashoka comes from Buddhist legends, which present him as a great, ideal king. These legends appear in texts that are not contemporary to Ashoka and were composed by Buddhist authors, who used various stories to illustrate the impact of their faith on Ashoka.

This makes it necessary to exercise caution while relying on them for historical information. Among modern scholars, opinions range from downright dismissal of these legends as mythological to acceptance of all historical portions that seem plausible. The Buddhist legends about Ashoka exist in several languages, including Sanskrit, Pali, Tibetan, Chinese, Burmese, Sinhala, Thai, Lao, and Khotanese. All these legends can be traced to two primary traditions: • the North Indian tradition preserved in the Sanskrit-language texts such as Divyavadana (including its constituent Ashokavadana); and Chinese sources such as A-yü wang chuan and A-yü wang ching. • the Sri Lankan tradition preserved in Pali-lanuage texts, such as Dipavamsa, Mahavamsa, Vamsatthapakasini (a commentary on Mahavamsa), Buddhaghosha's commentary on the Vinaya, and Samanta-pasadika. There are several significant differences between the two traditions. For example, the Sri Lankan tradition emphasizes Ashoka's role in convening the Third Buddhist council, and his dispatch of several missionaries to distant regions, including his son Mahinda to Sri Lanka. However, the North Indian tradition makes no mention of these events. It describes other events not found in the Sri Lankan tradition, such as a story about another son named Kunala. Even while narrating the common stories, the two traditions diverge in several ways. For example, both Ashokavadana and Mahavamsa mention that Ashoka's queen Tishyarakshita had the Bodhi Tree destroyed. In

Ashokavadana, the queen manages to have the tree healed after she realises her mistake. In the Mahavamsa, she permanently destroys the tree, but only after a branch of the tree has been transplanted in Sri Lanka. In another story, both the texts describe Ashoka's unsuccessful attempts to collect a relic of Gautama Buddha from Ramagrama.

Ashokavadana, he fails to do so because he cannot match the devotion of the Nagas who hold the relic; however, in the Mahavamsa, he fails to do so because the Buddha had destined the relic to be enshrined by King Dutthagamani of Sri Lanka. Using such stories, the Mahavamsa glorifies Sri Lanka as the new preserve of Buddhism. Other sources Numismatic, sculptural, and archaeological evidence supplements research on Ashoka.Ashoka's name appears in the lists of Mauryan kings in the various Puranas. However, these texts do not provide further details about him, as their Brahmanical authors were not patronised by the Mauryans. Other texts, such as the Arthashastra and Indica of Megasthenes, which provide general information about the Maurya period, can also be used to make inferences about Ashoka's reign.However, the Arthashastra is a normative text that focuses on an ideal rather than a historical state, and its dating to the Mauryan period is a subject of debate. The Indica is a lost work, and only parts of it survive in the form of paraphrases in later writings.The 12th-century text Rajatarangini mentions a Kashmiri king Ashoka of Gonandiya dynasty who built several stupas: some scholars, such as Aurel Stein, have identified this king with the Maurya king Ashoka; others, such as Ananda W. P. Guruge dismiss this identification as inaccurate.

Alternative interpretation of the epigraphic evidence The Edicts and their declared authors Edicts in the name of Piyadasi or Devanampiya Piyadasi ("King Piyadasi"): : Major Rock Edicts : Major Pillar Edicts Edicts in the name of Ashoka or just "Devanampiya" ("King"), or both together: : Minor Rock Edicts : Minor Pillar Edicts The different areas covered by the two types of inscriptions, and their different content in respect to Buddhism, may point to different rulers. [35] For some scholars such as Christopher I. Beckwith, Ashoka, whose name only appears in the Minor Rock Edicts, is not the same as king Piyadasi, or Devanampiya Piyadasi (i.e. "Beloved of the

Gods Piyadasi", "Beloved of the Gods" being a fairly widespread title for "King"), who is named as the author of the Major Pillar Edicts and the Major Rock Edicts. Beckwith suggests that Piyadasi was living in the 3rd century BCE, was probably the son of Chandragupta Maurya known to the Greeks as Amitrochates, and only advocated for piety ("Dharma") in his Major Pillar Edicts and Major Rock Edicts, without ever mentioning Buddhism, the Buddha or the Samgha (the single notable exception is the 7th Edict of the Major Pillar Edicts which does mention the Samgha, but is a considered a later fake by Beckwith). Also, the geographical spread of his inscription shows that Piyadasi ruled a vast Empire, contiguous with the Seleucid Empire in the West.

On the conNames and titles[edit] Names and titles of Ashoka "Devānampiyasa Asoka", in the Maski Edict of Ashoka. The name "Asoka" (A-so-ka) in the Maski Minor Rock Edict. Ashoka's title "Devanaṃpiyena Piyadasi" ( ) in the Lumbini Minor Pillar Edict. The name "A-shoka" literally means "without sorrow". According to an Ashokavadana legend, his mother gave him this name because his birth removed her sorrows. The name Priyadasi is associated with Ashoka in the 3rd–4th century CE Dipavamsa. The term literally means "he who regards amiably", or "of gracious mien" (Sanskrit: Priya-darshi). It may have been a regnal name adopted by Ashoka Ashoka's inscriptions mention his title Devanampiya (Sanskrit: Devanampriya, "Beloved of the Gods").

The identification of Devanampiya and Ashoka as the same person is established by the Maski and Gujarra inscriptions, which use both these terms for the king. The title was adopted by other kings, including the contemporary king Devanampiya Tissa of Anuradhapura and Ashoka's descendant Dasharatha Maurya. Date The Major Rock Edict No.13 of Ashoka, mentions the Greek kings Antiochus, Ptolemy, Antigonus, Magas and Alexander by name, as recipients of his teachings. The exact date of Ashoka's birth is not certain, as the extant contemporary Indian texts did not record such details. It is known that he lived in the 3rd century BCE, as his inscriptions mention several contemporary rulers whose dates are known with more certainty, such as Antiochus II Theos, Ptolemy II Philadelphus, Antigonus II Gonatas, Magas of Cyrene, and Alexander (of

Epirus or Corinth).

Thus, Ashoka must have been born sometime in the late 4th century BCE or early 3rd century BCE (c. 304 BCE), Pataliputra at the time of Ashoka Ruins of pillared hall at Kumrahar site at Pataliputra. The Pataliputra capital, 4th–3rd c. BCE. Ashoka was probably born in the city of Pataliputra. Remains of the city from around that time have been found through excavations in central areas of the modern city of Patna.

Ancestry Ashoka's own inscriptions are fairly detailed but make no mention of his ancestors. Other sources, such as the Puranas and the Mahavamsa state that his father was the Mauryan emperor Bindusara, and his grandfather was Chandragupta – the founder of the Empire. The Ashokavadana also names his father as Bindusara, but traces his ancestry to Buddha's contemporary king Bimbisara, through Ajatashatru, Udayin, Munda, Kakavarnin, Sahalin, Tulakuchi, Mahamandala, Prasenajit, and Nanda. The 16th century Tibetan monk Taranatha, whose account is a distorted version of the earlier traditions,describes Ashoka as the illegitimate son of king Nemita of Champarana from the daughter of a merchant.

Ashokavadana states that Ashoka's mother was the daughter of a Brahmin from Champa, and was prophesized to marry a king. Accordingly, her father took her to Pataliputra, where she was inducted into Bindusara's harem, and ultimately, became his chief queen.The Ashokavadana does not mention her by name, although other legends provide different names for her. For example, the Asokavadanamala calls her Subhadrangi.The Vamsatthapakasini or Mahavamsa-tika, a commentary on Mahavamsa, calls her "Dharma" ("Dhamma" in Pali), and states that she belonged to the Moriya Kshatriya clan. A Divyavadana legend calls her Janapada-kalyani;according to scholar Ananda W. P. Guruge, this is not a name, but an epithet.

THE STORY OF THE DIETIES

The story about the deities miraculously bringing weapons to Ashoka may be the text's way of deifying Ashoka; or indicating that Bindusara – who disliked Ashoka – wanted him to fail in Takshashila. Governor of Ujjain According to the Mahavamsa, Bindusara appointed Ashoka as the viceroy of present-day Ujjain which was an important administrative and commercial centre in the Avanti province of central India. This tradition is corroborated by the Saru Maru inscription discovered in central India; this inscription states that he visited the place as a prince. Ashoka's own rock edict mentions the presence of a prince viceroy at Ujjain during his reign, which further supports the tradition that he himself served as a viceroy at UjjainThe Saru Maru commemorative inscription seems to mention the presence of Ashoka in the area of Ujjain as he was still a Prince. Pataliputra was connected to Ujjain by multiple routes in Ashoka's time, and on the way, Ashoka entourage may have encamped at Rupnath, where his inscription has been found. According to the Sri Lankan tradition, Ashoka visited Vidisha, where he fell in love with a beautiful woman on his way to Ujjain. According to the Dipamvamsa and Mahamvamsa, the woman was Devi – the daughter of a merchant. According to the Mahabodhi-vamsa, she was Vidisha-Mahadevi and belonged to the Shakya clan of Gautama Buddha. The Buddhist chroniclers may have fabricated the Shakya connection to connect Ashoka's family to Buddha.The Buddhist texts allude to her being a Buddhist in her later years but do not describe her conversion to Buddhism. Therefore, it is likely that she was already a Buddhist when she met Ashoka. The Mahavamsa states that Devi gave birth to Ashoka's son Mahinda in Ujjain, and two years later, to a daughter named Sanghamitta. According to the Mahavamsa, Ashoka's son Mahinda was ordained at the age of 20 years, during the sixth year of Ashoka's reign. That means Mahinda must have been 14 years old when Ashoka ascended the throne. Even if Mahinda was born when Ashoka was as young as 20 years old, Ashoka must have ascended the throne at 34 years, which means he must have served as a viceroy for several years. Ascension to the throne Legends suggest that Ashoka was not the crown prince, and his ascension on the throne was disputed. .

??? ???

Contents

Printed by Libri Plureos GmbH in Hamburg,
Germany